# hampton roads 1862

first clash of the ironclads

ANGUS KONSTAM

# hampton roads 1862

## first clash of the ironclads

*Praeger Illustrated Military History Series*

Westport, Connecticut
London

**Library of Congress Cataloging-in-Publication Data**

Konstam, Angus.
    Hampton Roads 1862: clash of the ironclads / Angus Konstam.
        p. cm. – (Praeger illustrated military history, ISSN 1547-206X)
    Originally published: Oxford: Osprey, 2002.
    Includes bibliographical references and index.
    ISBN 0-275-98448-6 (alk. paper)
    1. Hampton Roads, Battle of, Va., 1862. I. Title. II. Series.
    E473.2.K66        2004
    973.7'52–dc22      2004050380

British Library Cataloguing in Publication Data is available.

First published in paperback in 2002 by Osprey Publishing Limited, Elms Court,
Chapel Way, Botley, Oxford OX2 9LP.  All rights reserved.

Copyright © 2004 by Osprey Publishing Limited

Library of Congress Catalog Card Number: 2004050380
ISBN: 0-275-98448-6
ISSN: 1547-206X

Praeger Publishers, 88 Post Road West, Westport, CT 06881
An imprint of Greenwood Publishing Group, Inc.
www.praeger.com

Printed in China through World Print Ltd.

The paper used in this book complies with the Permanent Paper Standard issued
by the National Information Standards Organization  (Z39.48-1984).

10  9  8  7  6  5  4  3  2  1

ILLUSTRATED BY: Adam Hook

# CONTENTS

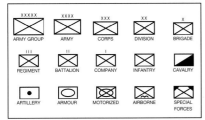

**KEY TO MILITARY SYMBOLS**

| XXXXX | XXXX | XXX | XX | X |
|-------|------|-----|-----|-----|
| ARMY GROUP | ARMY | CORPS | DIVISION | BRIGADE |
| III | II | I | | |
| REGIMENT | BATTALION | COMPANY | INFANTRY | CAVALRY |
| ARTILLERY | ARMOUR | MOTORIZED | AIRBORNE | SPECIAL FORCES |

# THE CONFEDERATE SEABOARD, MARCH–APRIL 1862

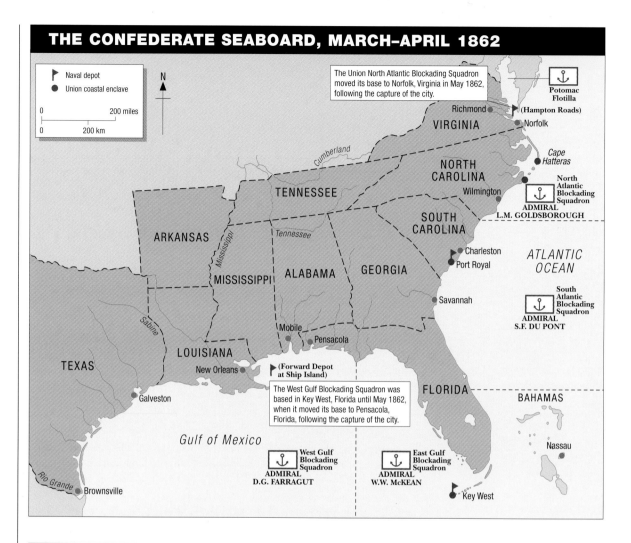

**Key:**
- Naval depot
- Union coastal enclave

N

0 — 200 miles
0 — 200 km

The Union North Atlantic Blockading Squadron moved its base to Norfolk, Virginia in May 1862, following the capture of the city.

Potomac Flotilla

Richmond
(Hampton Roads)
Norfolk

**VIRGINIA**

Cumberland

Cape Hatteras

**NORTH CAROLINA**

Wilmington

North Atlantic Blockading Squadron
ADMIRAL L.M. GOLDSBOROUGH

**TENNESSEE**

**ARKANSAS**

Mississippi

Tennessee

**SOUTH CAROLINA**

Charleston
Port Royal

*ATLANTIC OCEAN*

**MISSISSIPPI**

**ALABAMA**

**GEORGIA**

Savannah

South Atlantic Blockading Squadron
ADMIRAL S.F. DU PONT

Sabine

Mobile
Pensacola

**LOUISIANA**

New Orleans

(Forward Depot at Ship Island)

**TEXAS**

Galveston

The West Gulf Blockading Squadron was based in Key West, Florida until May 1862, when it moved its base to Pensacola, Florida, following the capture of the city.

**FLORIDA**

**BAHAMAS**

*Gulf of Mexico*

Nassau

West Gulf Blockading Squadron
ADMIRAL D.G. FARRAGUT

East Gulf Blockading Squadron
ADMIRAL W.W. McKEAN

Rio Grande
Brownsville

Key West

# INTRODUCTION

On 9 March 1862, the world's first battle between two ironclad warships took place in the confined waters of Hampton Roads, Virginia. Thousands of soldiers and civilians lined the shores to watch the Confederate casemate ironclad CSS *Virginia* and the Union turreted ironclad USS *Monitor*, which resembled no warships any of the onlookers had seen before. The previous day, the crew of the *Virginia* had demonstrated the vulnerability of wooden warships when faced by an armored opponent. She sank two Union warships, and left others stranded, vulnerable to attack the following day. During the night the tiny *Monitor* reinforced the battered Union fleet, so that when the *Virginia* sortied the following morning, the *Monitor* steamed out to meet her. Although the ensuing four-hour duel was a stalemate, with neither side causing any significant damage or even causing a fatality, the Confederate attempt to break the Union blockade of the Southern coastline had been thwarted. It can be argued that the stalemate at Hampton Roads ultimately led to the defeat of the Confederacy, as the Union naval blockade gradually bled the country of the means of defense. The battle was also a triumph for the naval designers who produced the two warships. In a single day, they had demonstrated that all unarmored wooden warships were obsolete, and the future of seapower lay in the creation of ironclad warships. As a result, the Battle of Hampton Roads has rightly been seen as a turning point in naval history.

When the Southern States seceded from the Union in 1861, neither the US Navy nor the nascent Confederate Navy was prepared for what was to follow. The Union had a handful of warships with which to institute a blockade of thousands of miles of enemy coastline, while the Confederates had no warships at all with which to defend themselves. Confederate Secretary of the Navy Stephen R. Mallory set into motion the train of events that culminated in the duel between the ironclads that morning in Hampton Roads. He decided that the best way to use the limited resources available to the Confederate Navy was the creation of a fleet of ironclad warships. Following the capture of the US Naval Yard in Portsmouth across the river from Norfolk, Virginia, the means to create a prototype ironclad were presented to him. Mallory and his advisors decided to raise the burned-out hulk of the steam frigate USS *Merrimac*, which lay in the Elizabeth River, and then convert her into an armored warship. When news of this work reached Washington, Union Secretary of the Navy Gideon Welles was allocated funds to create a Union ironclad to match the *Merrimac*. The result was the USS *Monitor*. From the moment work began on the *Monitor*, it was inevitable that the two warships would meet in battle. The result was the Battle of Hampton Roads. Participants and onlookers alike were well aware of the importance of the clash. At stake were the fate of the Union naval blockade and ultimately the survival of the Confederacy.

LEFT **The battle between the CSS *Virginia* and the USS *Monitor* on 9 March 1862 was the first naval engagement between two ironclad warships, and represented a turning point in naval history. *The Monitor and the Merrimac*, oil on canvas by Xanthus R. Smith. (Union League of Philadelphia, Philadelphia, PA)**

# CHRONOLOGY

## 1861

**17 April:** Virginia secedes from the Union
**19 April:** Norfolk Navy Yard abandoned, and *Merrimac* destroyed
**23 June:** Plans proposed for conversion of the hulk of the *Merrimac* into an ironclad
**4 October:** John Ericsson signs contract to build the *Monitor*

## 1862

**30 January:** *Monitor* launched
**17 February:** CSS *Virginia* commissioned
**25 February:** USS *Monitor* commissioned
**6 March:** *Monitor* begins journey to Hampton Roads

### 8 March: Battle of Hampton Roads (First Day)
10.00hrs: The French sloop *Gassendi* prepares to move, raising the suspicions of General Wool
10.30: Flag Officer Buchanan orders the CSS *Virginia* be prepared for sea
11.00: The *Virginia* begins her journey down the Elizabeth River
11.15: Union signal station on Newport News Point sights smoke on the Elizabeth River
11.30: General Mansfield alerts General Wool to the possibility that the *Virginia* may be approaching
12.00: The *Virginia* approaches the mouth of the Elizabeth River
12.45: Union fleet sees the *Virginia* and her consorts off Sewell's Point
12.55: The tug *Zouave* is sent to investigate the Confederate naval activity
13.20: The tug *Zouave* opens fire on the *Virginia*
13.30: The *Minnesota*, *St. Lawrence* and *Roanoke* get under way, heading for Newport News Point
14.00: The tug *Beaufort* fires on the USS *Congress*
14.10: The Confederate batteries on Sewell's Point exchange fire with the Union flotilla
14.20: The *Virginia* and the *Congress* exchange fire
14.30: The *Virginia* closes to within 30 yards of the *Congress*
14.50: Leaving the battered *Congress*, the *Virginia* steers toward the *Cumberland*
15.05: The *Virginia* rams the *Cumberland*
15.10: The USS *Minnesota* and the *St. Lawrence* run aground
15.15: The *Virginia* withdraws, then rams the *Cumberland* a second time
15.20: The *Cumberland* sinks, and the *Virginia* commences her 180-degree turn
15.30: The James River Squadron begins its run past the Newport News batteries
15.45: The CSS *Patrick Henry* is hit by fire from shore batteries
16.10: The *Virginia* returns, and rakes the *Congress*
17.00: The *Congress* surrenders
17.10: Confederate vessels approaching the *Congress* come under fire from sharpshooters
17.35: Flag Officer Buchanan wounded
17.45: Heated shot fired at the *Congress*
18.00: Jones steams toward the *Minnesota*
18.30: The attack is abandoned, and the *Virginia* heads back toward Sewell's Point
19.45: The *Virginia* and her escorts anchor under the guns of Sewell's Point

### 9 March: Battle of Hampton Roads (Second Day)
00.30: The *Congress* explodes
05.00: Flag Officer Buchanan and other wounded sent ashore

06.00: The *Virginia* slips her moorings then waits off Sewell's Point for the fog to clear. The *Minnesota* prepares for action

08.00: The *Virginia* and her consorts steam into Hampton Roads

08.10: The *Monitor* heads south to intercept

08.25: The *Minnesota* and the *Virginia* exchange shots

08.35: The *Monitor* and the *Virginia* commence their duel, which continues for the next two hours

10.55: Lieutenant Worden in the *Monitor* attempts to ram the *Virginia*

11.05: The *Monitor* retires to shallow water to replenish her ammunition supplies

11.10: The *Virginia* steers toward the *Minnesota*

11.30: The *Monitor* returns to the battle, and attempts to ram the *Virginia* again

11.35: The *Virginia* runs aground, and the *Monitor* lies alongside the *Virginia* and fires at her

11.40: Jones signals his consorts to come to his aid, but the *Virginia* pulls herself off the shoal, and her consorts return to Sewell's Point

12.05: The *Virginia* attempts to ram and board the *Monitor*

12.10: Shot from *Virginia* hits the *Monitor's* pilot house, wounding Worden

12.15: Lieutenant Greene takes over command of the *Monitor*. He withdraws from the fight

12.30: The *Virginia* steams toward the *Minnesota* for a final attack

12.40: Attempt abandoned due to falling water levels

13.05: Jones holds a council of war then elects to return to his moorings off Sewell's Point, ending the engagement

13.30: The *Virginia* moors off Sewell's Point, while the *Monitor* anchors off Fort Monroe

**21 March:** Flag Officer Tattnal appointed to command *Virginia*

**9 May:** Fall of Norfolk

**11 May:** Destruction of the *Virginia*

**15 May:** Engagement at Drewry's Bluff

**31 December:** *Monitor* sinks during a gale off Cape Hatteras, North Carolina

**Few accurate depictions of the conflict exist, and although this late 19th-century rendition placed the *Minnesota* too close to the action and placed an incorrect ensign on the spar deck of the *Virginia*, it is an otherwise reasonably accurate depiction. (Mariners)**

# OPPOSING COMMANDERS

## UNION

### Gideon Welles, Secretary of the Navy (1802–79)

Born in Connecticut, Welles became the owner and editor of the *Hartford Times* newspaper in 1826. The same year he won a seat in the Connecticut Legislature that he held for nine years. In 1846 he began a four-year term in the Navy Department as the Chief of the Bureau of Provisions and Clothing, which provided him with a modicum of understanding of the Navy and its organization. In 1850 he failed to win a seat on the Senate as a Democrat, so he promptly switched to the Republican Party. In 1856 he founded the *Hartford Evening Press*, but failed in a bid to become Governor of Connecticut. When Abraham Lincoln became President in 1860, he appointed Welles to his cabinet, and in March 1861 he became the Secretary of the Navy, a post he held throughout the war. He quickly demonstrated the ability to select gifted subordinates, and under his tenure the Navy Department grew to meet its new wartime responsibilities. Welles worked hard to expand and modernize the navy, and pressed through the introduction of ironclads into naval service, while masterminding the blockade of the Confederate coastline. He was a staunch advocate of Ericsson and his monitor design, particularly after Hampton Roads. Welles was also a loyal supporter of the President throughout his term, but he still argued with Lincoln over several issues, such as press censorship and individual rights. In 1869 he retired from political life to write his memoirs.

Gideon Welles, the Union Secretary of the Navy was a former newspaper owner and an experienced politician. Although initially sceptical of Ericsson's design, he later became a whole-hearted supporter of the *Monitor* design. (Hensley)

### John Ericsson, Designer of the USS *Monitor* (1803–89)

Born in Sweden, the young Ericsson was an engineer in the Swedish Army, but left for Britain in 1826 to promote his design for an engine. Although his machine evoked little interest, he stayed on, and in 1837 he built a twin-screwed steamboat, powered by his own propellers and engines. In 1839 he emigrated to the United States, where he began work on a steam warship for the US Navy. Ericsson fell from favor five years later when a fatal ordnance explosion occurred on his experimental warship. He concentrated on developing an ironclad turret warship, but as the Navy refused to deal with him, he tried unsuccessfully to sell his design to the French. Following the outbreak of the Civil War, Ericsson completed his design for his warship, and was encouraged by supporters to submit the plans to the Navy Department. After initial reluctance, the Navy decided to award Ericsson a contract to build his ironclad, which was completed in February 1862. Ericsson named her *Monitor*, and following her success at the Battle of Hampton Roads in March, the name was adopted by a succession of subsequent ironclads of similar type, many of which were designed by Ericsson. His patented turret

John Ericsson, the Swedish-born designer of the USS *Monitor* was plagued by criticism until the vessel's baptism of fire. Although his design had flaws, "Ericsson's Folly" proved her worth during the battle. (Mariners)

Lieutenant John Latimer Worden USN commanded the USS *Monitor* from her commissioning in Brooklyn until the final stages of the battle, when he was wounded. He demonstrated a remarkable coolness under fire, and good tactical ability. (Mariners)

design was used in most Union monitors throughout the war, and after the conflict his designs were copied or commissioned by several other navies. He continued to design new naval vessels and experiment with propulsion systems until his death.

### Lieutenant John L. Worden, Commanding Officer of the USS *Monitor* (1818–97)

Born in New York, Worden entered the US Navy as a midshipman in 1835, and by 1846 he had reached the rank of lieutenant. He served both at sea and ashore until the outbreak of the war, when he was sent to Fort Pickens, Georgia. His orders were to encourage the garrison there to hold their fort until relieved, but during his return journey he was captured. Worden was exchanged as a prisoner of war in October, and on his return he was selected to command the experimental ironclad *Monitor*, then under construction in New York.

Following the battle, Worden recovered from his wounds in Washington, D.C., where he and his crew received the Thanks of Congress. He was promoted to the rank of Commander in July 1862, and he became a Captain in February 1863, when he was given command of the monitor USS *Montauk*. He destroyed the Confederate raider *Nashville* on Georgia's Ogeechee River and then his monitor participated in the bombardment of Fort Sumter in April. In May he returned to Washington, where he was attached to the Navy Department, tasked with advising on the development of new monitors. Following the end of the war he commanded the USS *Pensacola*, and became the Superintendent of the Naval Academy in 1870. He was promoted to the rank of Rear-Admiral, and commanded the European Squadron and served ashore until his retirement in 1886, after a half-century of service.

### Lieutenant Samuel D. Greene, Executive Officer of the USS *Monitor* (1839–84)

Greene graduated from the US Naval Academy, Annapolis, in his native Maryland in 1859, and served as a midshipman aboard the USS *Hartford* in the Far East until the outbreak of the war, when the ship returned to the United States. He was promoted to lieutenant in 1861, and he duly volunteered for service on board the USS *Monitor*, then under construction. As the Executive Officer, his duty was to command the turret of the ironclad, and during the Battle of Hampton Roads he used his initiative and common sense to develop a way to use the turret and its guns to best effect. When Lieutenant Worden was wounded during the closing stages of the battle, Greene assumed command of the *Monitor*, and continued to hold the post until Commander John Bankhead was sent to relieve him. His decision not to pursue the *Virginia* and continue the battle preyed on him in later years.

Greene was a highly-strung officer, and although he served with distinction for the remainder of the war, and was eventually promoted to Commander in 1872, his guilt never left him. In December 1884, while serving as the Executive Officer in the Portsmouth Navy Yard in Maine, he put a pistol to his head, reputedly while "in a state of high nervous excitement," and killed himself. One historian argued that Greene's suicide was directly linked to the first duel between two ironclads, and the battle's only fatality.

Lieutenant Dana Greene USN was the Executive Officer of the USS *Monitor* during the battle. He supervised operations from the turret, and took over command of the vessel when his commanding officer was wounded. (Mariners)

# CONFEDERATE

### Stephen R. Mallory, Secretary of the Navy (1812–73)

Although he was born in Trinidad, Mallory was brought up in Key West, Florida, where he served as a customs inspector and port administrator. Trained as a lawyer, he became a local judge in 1840, and in 1851 he became a Florida senator. He served on the Naval Affairs Committee until the secession of Florida from the Union. He offered his services to the Confederate President Jefferson Davis, who appointed him Confederate Secretary of the Navy in May 1861. He held the position throughout the war, and was instrumental in developing new technologies to help offset Union naval superiority. These included the development of an ironclad fleet, torpedoes (mines), and rifled ordnance. In late 1861 he approved plans to raise the burned-out hulk of the USS *Merrimac* and to convert her into a casemate ironclad (the *Virginia*), and closely supervised the development of the project. The success of the design was an affirmation of Mallory's belief in ironclads.

A gifted politician and administrator, Mallory proved himself capable of dealing with the technical and logistical challenges of his job. Although his strategic vision of the *Virginia*'s ability to break the Union blockade was flawed, his reliance on developing a fleet of ironclads helped protect the major ports of the Confederacy for as long as practicable. Following the collapse of the Confederacy he was arrested and imprisoned for a year. After the war he moved to Pensacola where he practised law until his death.

Stephen Russell Mallory, the Confederate Secretary of the Navy. He was instrumental in developing an ironclad fleet to protect the Confederacy, and the *Virginia* was the prototype for this ambitious program. (Monroe County Public Library. Key West, FL)

### John L. Porter, principal designer of the CSS *Virginia* (1821–84)

Porter was brought up in Portsmouth, Virginia, where his father owned a civilian shipyard close to the Norfolk Naval Yard. He was duly hired by the US Navy Department as a civilian naval designer, and worked on several projects in the Navy Department, including the development of steam warships. In 1859 he was appointed Naval Constructor, the leading warship design post in the Navy. When Virginia seceded in 1861, Porter resigned his post and returned to Virginia. For a few months he served on the staff of the Virginia State Navy, but following its amalgamation into the new Confederate Navy he joined the offices of the Navy Department in Richmond. Although he held no official position until 1864, he was de facto head of naval construction in the Department. Together with ordnance expert Lieutenant John M. Brooke and engineer William P. Williamson, Porter drew up plans for the conversion of the burned-out warship *Merrimac* into a Confederate ironclad. Although there was a degree of animosity between Porter and Brooke, the trio succeeded in converting the warship that was to become the casemate ironclad CSS *Virginia*.

Following the success of his design, Porter was authorized to develop plans for several new ironclads, including the highly successful *Richmond* Class. He continued to design the majority of new warships in the Confederacy, although his position as Chief Naval Constructor was only officially ratified in 1864. An extremely gifted designer, Porter became a businessman after the war.

Naval Constructor John L. Porter developed plans to convert the burnt-out remains of the *Merrimac* into the powerful casemate ironclad *Virginia*. He achieved miracles, given the limited resources available in the Confederacy. (Mariners)

Flag Officer Franklin Buchanan was a native of Maryland, who cast his lot with the Confederacy. A skilled naval tactician and administrator, he commanded his flagship the CSS *Virginia* during her attack on the *Cumberland* and *Congress*. (LoC)

## Flag Officer Franklin Buchanan, Commanding Officer of the CSS *Virginia* (1800–74)

Born in Maryland, Buchanan entered the US Navy in 1815, and gradually rose through the ranks, being promoted Commander in 1841. He assisted in the creation of the US Naval Academy at Annapolis, and in 1845 he became its first superintendent. He commanded the sloop USS *Germantown* during the Mexican-American War (1846–48), and in 1855 he was promoted to Captain and placed in command of the Washington Navy Yard. In 1861 he thought it certain that Maryland would secede from the Union, and he resigned from the Navy. When it transpired that Maryland remained loyal, Buchanan tried to withdraw his resignation, but the Navy Department refused his request. Consequently in August 1861 Buchanan headed south to offer his services to the Confederacy. He was appointed Captain in September, and served in the Navy Department, masterminding the drive to create a Confederate Navy from scratch. In February 1862 he was made Flag Officer, and given command of naval forces in Virginia. His decision to use his flagship the CSS *Virginia* to attack the Union blockading fleet in Hampton Roads initiated the Battle of Hampton Roads. He was wounded in the action, but was rewarded by promotion to full Admiral in August. He subsequently commanded the defenses of Mobile, Alabama, and during the Battle of Mobile Bay (August 1864) his flagship was the ironclad CSS *Tennessee*. After the war he worked as an insurance executive in Maryland until his death.

## Lieutenant Catesby ap R. Jones, Executive Officer of the CSS *Virginia* (1821–77)

Born in Virginia, Jones entered the US Navy in 1836, and served in the Pacific before attending the Philadelphia Naval School, where he passed as midshipman in 1841. He then was posted to the Navy Department's Hydrographical Office, and he performed survey work off the Florida coast for several years. In 1853 Lieutenant Jones was assigned to the Washington Navy Yard, where he assisted John A. Dahlgren in developing a new system of smoothbore ordnance. He also served as gunnery officer on the USS *Merrimac*. When Virginia seceded in 1861 he resigned his commission and became a lieutenant in the Confederate Navy. He was appointed to the *Merrimac* during her conversion into the CSS *Virginia*, and Jones played a major role in preparing the ironclad for active service. During the first day of the Battle of Hampton Roads, Flag Officer Buchanan was wounded, and Jones assumed command of the Virginia in time for her duel with the USS *Monitor*, fighting her with skill. He continued as the *Virginia*'s Executive Officer until the vessel's destruction in May. By 1863 he had been promoted and was placed in charge of the Navy's Ordnance Works in Selma, Alabama. He settled there after the war, and became a businessman until his death in a quarrel. Jones remains the unsung hero of Hampton Roads, and historians have only recently acknowledged his true influence on the events of March 1862.

Lieutenant Catesby ap Roger Jones, CSN was the Executive Officer of the CSS *Virginia*. He commanded the ironclad during her famous battle with the USS *Monitor*, as Flag Officer Buchanan was wounded during the previous day's fighting. (Mariners)

# OPPOSING FORCES

## CONFEDERATE

### CSS *Virginia*

The decision to build an ironclad from the hulk of the burned-out steam frigate USS *Merrimac* was made by Stephen Mallory, the Confederate Secretary of the Navy. He realized that it was almost impossible for his Navy to break the Union blockade by conventional means, so he adopted a more radical approach, placing his faith in ironclads and rifled ordnance. The *Merrimac* had been burned and sunk when Union forces withdrew from Norfolk, but on inspection she was deemed to still be valuable. Although her upper works had been destroyed, her engines were salvageable, and her lower hull remained in good condition. The hulk was raised and brought into a dry dock in the Navy Yard for conversion. Mallory gathered a design team to work on the project. It consisted of leading naval constructor, John L. Porter, the ordnance expert John M. Brooke and naval engineer William P. Williamson – three of the best designers in the Confederacy. Given the lack of manufacturing capacity in the South, all three men realized that any attempt to produce a technically challenging design was beyond the abilities of Southern foundries. Following a series of meetings, Porter, Brooke and Williamson decided that the conversion of the burned-out hull of the *Merrimac* was far from ideal, as the vessel was cumbersome, and its engines were underpowered. Its principal advantage was that it allowed an ironclad to be built faster than if it were constructed from scratch. Mallory's directive to start work on the ironclad was issued on 11 June 1861, and she was commissioned into service just eight months later, on 17 February 1862. Given the limited industrial capacity of the Southern states, this represented an incredible accomplishment. The

**The CSS *Virginia* was not completed when she fought the USS *Monitor*. She carried the wrong ammunition, and the gun port shutters designed to protect her gun crews were still not fitted. (Hensley)**

The two 11in. Dahlgren smoothbore guns carried in the USS *Monitor* weighed 15,700lb, and fired a 165lb solid cast-iron roundshot or a 136lb conical shell. While Dahlgren limited their propellant to 15lb of powder, subsequent tests proved the barrels could withstand larger charges. (Author's Collection)

Confederacy lacked sufficient engineering plants, skilled workers and raw materials, and Porter and his team continually modified their design to suit the manufacturing capacity available to them. The main elements required were wood, rolled iron sheet for the armor plating, a propulsion system, and reliable ordnance. Wood was in plentiful supply, although the ramshackle rail infrastructure made the transport of shipbuilding lumber and metal plates a continual problem. Porter relied on the Tredegar Iron Works in Richmond, Virginia, to supply metal plates. Although the Richmond foundry was the largest ironworks in the Confederacy, it was small in comparison to its northern counterparts. The initial contract specified the use of 1in. iron plates, but tests conducted by John M. Brooke at Jamestown proved that a series of one-inch layers would be inadequate protection for the ironclad. Ironically, this was precisely the form of plating fitted to the USS *Monitor*, but she relied on eight layers of 1in. plate to protect her turret, twice the armor available to the *Virginia*'s designers. The vessel was finally protected with two layers of 2in. iron plate, and the Tredegar Works had to alter their machinery so it could roll the thicker plate, which delayed production, but the thicker metal greatly improved the defensive qualities of the vessel. It was bolted to the wooden backing by applying an inner horizontal belt and an outer vertical one. As for a propulsion system, Williamson oversaw the stripping and refurbishment of the *Merrimac*'s engines. Although underpowered, they were reliable, available, and could be fitted into the ironclad with minimal delay.

The basic design of the Confederate ironclad relied on a wooden casemate (shield) with rounded ends, erected on top of the existing hull. When coated with metal plate, this gave the warship the ungainly

Lieutenant John Mercer Brooke, CSN was one of the most able ordnance designers in America. He worked with John Porter on the design of the *Virginia*, modifying her armament and armor to reflect the latest developments in artillery. (Hensley)

The CSS *Patrick Henry* was the flagship of the James River Squadron. On 8 March the well-proportioned sidewheel steamer ran past the Union batteries on Newport News under cover of fire from the *Virginia*. (Mariners)

appearance of an upturned bath. The wood was approximately 2ft thick and the casemate sloped inward at a 35-degree angle, which Brooke determined was the best to deflect enemy shot. The armor extended from the top of the casemate down to the lower hull and beyond, ending 6in. below the waterline. The decision to extend the armor below the point where the casemate joined the hull (known as the "knuckle") added weight to the vessel, and sacrificed maneuverability for protection, but it made the vessel virtually impervious to enemy shot. The upper spar deck (or "hurricane deck") on top of the casemate was unarmored, and fitted with ventilation grilles. The lower hull itself was all but submerged, offering virtually no target to the enemy, although on the second day of the battle more of it was exposed than had been the previous day. The ironclad had used up coal, and her bunkers were not replenished during the night of 8/9 March. Consequently, she rode higher in the water, exposing part of her lower hull below the protective "knuckle".

The ironclad's armament consisted of six 9in. Dahlgren smoothbore guns (part of the *Merrimac*'s original armament) plus two new 6.4in. Brooke rifled guns mounted as broadside weapons on conventional carriages. All these pieces were mounted on conventional carriages, and fired out of broadside ports, In addition, two 7in. Brooke rifles on pivot mounts were fitted at the bow and stern, so they could fire ahead, astern or at an angle out of the corner of the casemate. In theory, the ironclad had the capability of all-round fire, although her real strength lay in the power of her broadside armament. An even more potent offensive weapon was the 1,500lb cast-iron ram fitted to the bow, three feet below the waterline.

Christened the CSS *Virginia*, she was commissioned days before the battle, but she was still unfinished when Admiral Buchanan decided to use her to attack the Union blockading fleet. Much internal work remained to be done, her gunport shutters had not been fitted, and she lacked sufficient stores to allow her to remain at sea for more than a day

or two. There were still problems with her rudder, and it was estimated the cumbersome vessel would take almost 30 minutes to complete a 180-degree turn. Despite her lack of speed, poor maneuverability and a large draught (23ft), she was a powerful warship. She was also more than a match for all the Union vessels in Hampton Roads combined, until the arrival of her ironclad rival in time for the second day of the battle.

**CSS *Virginia*'s Officers**
Commanding Officer: Flag Officer Franklin Buchanan
Executive Officer: Lieutenant Catesby ap Roger Jones
Chief Engineering Officer: Lieutenant Ramsay
Lieutenants (6), Midshipmen (7)
Captain of Marines: Lieutenant Thom
Surgeon: Dinwiddie Phillips
Paymaster: James Semple

### The James River Squadron

Waiting for the opportunity to pass through the Union fleet off Hampton Roads and slip into Norfolk was the James River Squadron; a collection of three wooden gunboats, under the command of Commander John R. Tucker. Tucker was the Commanding Officer of the sidewheel gunboat CSS *Patrick Henry*, a beautiful vessel that was formerly called *Yorktown*. She went on to become the Confederate Navy's training ship. She was accompanied by her sister ship the CSS *Jamestown* (commanded by Lieutenant Joseph M. Barney) and the small gunboat CSS *Teaser* (commanded by Lieutenant William A. Webb). At the start of

**One of the Confederate batteries built in 1861 to defend Norfolk and its hinterland. Batteries such as this were created on Sewell's Point, Pig Point, and Craney Island to cover the river approaches to the city. (LoV)**

The gunners manning the Confederate batteries on Sewell's Point watch as the *Virginia* and her escorts return from their sortie on 8 March. The soldiers had an ideal vantage point to watch both days of the fighting. (Hensley)

the battle Tucker's squadron was moored off Jamestown, several miles up the James River from the Union fleet. They came under the overall command of Flag Officer Buchanan, who ordered Tucker to be ready to support the *Virginia* on the morning of 8 March 1862. All of the squadron's ships were converted merchant vessels, and lacked the strength to fight the more powerful Union warships on their own.

### The *Virginia*'s escorts

The *Virginia* was supported by two small tugboats, which were based at Portsmouth or Norfolk. Their sole purpose was to tow the ironclad safely up the Elizabeth River into Hampton Roads, then to cut her loose. After that they were to stand by under the protection of the guns on Sewell's Point in case Buchanan required any further assistance. Both the CSS *Raleigh* and the CSS *Beaufort* were puny vessels, incapable of posing any threat to the Union fleet. Both vessels had escaped the Confederate defeat at Roanoke Island in February, and the subsequent destruction of the Confederate wooden gunboat squadron at Elizabeth City. They were both small enough to escape up the Dismal Swamp Canal to the safety of Norfolk, and were duly attached to Buchanan's "Chesapeake Bay Squadron", the grandly imposing name given to the motley collection of gunboats that sought refuge from the Union blockade behind the guns surrounding Norfolk. They were commanded by Lieutenant William L. Parker, who was also Captain of the *Beaufort*.

### The Defenses of Norfolk

The Confederates, who had approximately 9,000 troops in the area, held the southern side of Hampton Roads. They came under the jurisdiction of Major General Benjamin Huger, commander of the Department of Norfolk, although in theory Flag Officer Buchanan was the senior officer there. Huger was also supposed to work in concert with the 12,000 troops screening the Union forces around

Fort Monroe and Newport News, who were commanded by Major General John B. Magruder. In reality, Huger was an independent commander, and the lack of communication between the Confederate Army and Navy in Norfolk would have severe repercussions. The Portsmouth–Norfolk–Gosport area was of major strategic importance to the Confederates, as the area housed the Confederacy's main naval base, and Norfolk was one of the largest cities in Virginia. It was, therefore, well defended, and Confederate batteries dominated the southern shore of Hampton Roads. These emplacements were sited on Sewell's Point, at the eastern mouth of the Elizabeth River, on Craney Island, blocking the river approaches to Norfolk, and further to the west, where the batteries protected both Norfolk and Suffolk. Further batteries lined the western shore of the Elizabeth River, between Sewell's Point and Norfolk. Magruder had his headquarters in the fortification immediately north of Norfolk. These troops manning the batteries and redoubts had an unobstructed view of the battle, and observers on Sewell's Point were ideally placed to watch both phases of the conflict, and to offer protection to the *Virginia* when required.

## CONFEDERATE VESSELS

**CSS *VIRGINIA*** – Casemate Screw Ram (Armored)
**Built:** Boston 1855, converted Norfolk 1861–62. **Commissioned:** March 1862
**Dimensions:** 263ft (length) x 51ft 4in. (beam) x 22ft (draft)
**Armament:** 2 x 7in. rifles, 6 x 9in. smoothbores, 2 x 6.4in. rifles
**Armor:** 4in., with timber backing
**Complement:** 320
**Speed:** 8 knots

**CSS *PATRICK HENRY*, CSS *JAMESTOWN*** – Wooden Sidewheel Gunboats
(Unarmored)
**Built:** New York, 1853 [both]. **Commissioned:** April 1861
**Dimensions:** 250ft x 34ft x 13ft. **Displacement:** 1,300 tons
**Armament:** (*Patrick Henry*) 1 x 10in. smoothbore, 1 x 64-pdr. smoothbore, 6 x 8in. smoothbores, 2 x 32-pdr. rifles. Although details are unknown, the *Jamestown* was probably similarly armed, although she only carried 2 x 8in. smoothbores.
**Complement:** 150
**Speed:** 12 knots

**CSS *TEASER*** – Wooden Screw Tug (Unarmored)
**Built:** Philadelphia, c.1855. **Commissioned:** 1861
**Dimensions:** 80ft x 18ft x 7ft. **Displacement:** 65 tons
**Armament:** 1 x 32-pdr. rifle
**Complement:** 25
**Speed:** 10 knots

**CSS *BEAUFORT*** – Wooden Screw Tugboat (Unarmored)
**Built:** Wilmington, DE, c.1854. **Commissioned:** July 1861
**Dimensions:** 85ft x 17ft 6in. x 7ft. **Displacement:** 85 tons
**Armament:** 1 x 32-pdr. rifle
**Complement:** approx. 25
**Speed:** 9 knots

**CSS *RALEIGH*** – Iron Screw Tugboat (Unarmored)
**Built:** Not recorded. **Commissioned:** May 1861
**Dimensions:** 80ft x 18ft x 7ft. **Displacement:** 65 tons
**Armament:** 2 x 6-pdr. howitzers
**Complement:** approx. 20
**Speed:** Not recorded

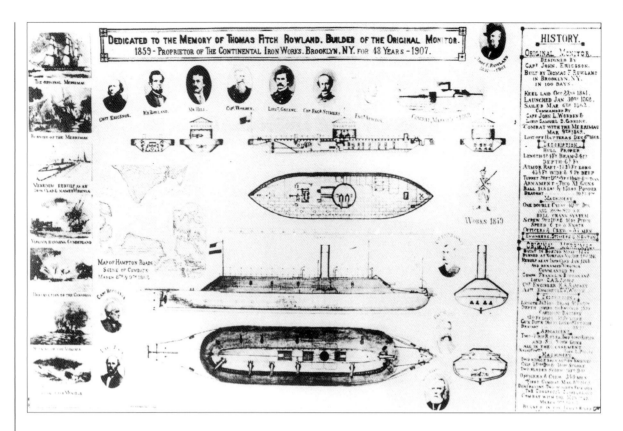

# UNION

### USS *Monitor*

When reports reached Washington that the Confederates were building an ironclad warship, the Navy Department became alarmed, and lobbied for funds to counter the threat with their own ironclad program. Gideon Welles, the Secretary of the Navy, was a highly experienced and competent administrator, but so far his efforts had been concentrated on expanding the navy by ordering new conventional warships and converting merchantmen for naval service. His primary aim was to create an effective blockade of the Confederacy, and the *Merrimac* threatened to break this maritime stranglehold. Congress was equally perturbed, and allocated funds for the creation of ironclads within days. Welles founded an "Ironclad Board", charged with examining proposals for ironclads, and following an appeal for designs the board retired to select the most promising. Three were chosen; a casemate ironclad similar to the French *Gloire* which became known as the USS *New Ironsides*, a small armored gunboat which became the USS *Galena*, and the revolutionary design proposed by Swedish-born designer John Ericsson for a turreted ironclad. This last vessel would become the USS *Monitor*. The Board was initially hesitant to approve Ericsson's design, as his vessel looked like no warship that had ever been seen before. One Board member even tried to force Ericsson to add masts and sails to the design, but the inventor refused. At a time when naval technology was being transformed, advocates of older, more traditional methods of ship construction were resistant to change.

A poster dedicated to Thomas F. Rowland of the Continental Iron Works gives a good impression of the difference in size between the two ironclads. Commissioned almost four decades after the battle, it emphasized the new spirit of unity in the nation by honoring the participants of both sides. (Hensley)

One of three sail-powered warships to participate in the battle, the USS *St. Lawrence* carried 44 guns. She ran aground during the afternoon of 8 March, but unlike her consort the *Minnesota*, the frigate could be refloated. (Mariners)

Ericsson's design was for a small armored hull to be fitted with a revolving gun turret containing two smoothbore guns. These guns were to be protected by eight layers of 1in. iron plate, bent into a curve to create the shape of the turret. The hull was constructed in two parts, the upper portion sitting on top of the lower hull like a raft. This upper part was protected by two ½in. deck plates laid over the deck beams, which provided little protection to fire from above, but as the design was meant to be a response to the threat of a Confederate ironclad, this was not considered a problem.

The sides of the hull were protected by 5in. of side armor in five 1in. strips, backed by just over 2ft of oak. When the guns were fitted and all the crew and stores embarked, the freeboard of the ironclad was less than 18in., which meant she was only capable of operating in calm coastal waters. It also meant that the hull presented an almost impossibly small target for enemy gunners. The hull was flat bottomed, and the upper portion of the hull extended over the lower part, protecting the rudder and screw. Unlike the *Virginia*, which had a draft of 22ft, Ericsson's ironclad could operate in less than 11ft of water.

She was powered by Ericsson's own "vibrating-lever" engines, which gave her a top speed of around 6 knots. A smaller engine powered the turret's rotation mechanism, which was controlled by an engineer inside the turret using a clutch mechanism. In theory, the 120-ton, 20ft diameter turret could rotate through 360 degrees in 24 seconds. It turned on a heavy central spindle, and to turn the whole device was elevated a few inches off the deck, so it effectively sat on the spindle's central column. Designed to house two powerful 15in. Dahlgren smoothbores, the turret was fitted with 11in. Dahlgrens instead, as the production of the larger guns was plagued by problems. The smaller 11in. pieces were available immediately, and were proven to be effective. Iron shutters known as "port stoppers" could be lowered over the gunports by means of pulleys inside the gun turret when the guns were not in use, or to protect the gunners from enemy fire.

When she was completed, the little ironclad was 179ft long, with a beam of 41¼ft. Although newspapermen had dubbed her "Ericsson's folly", the ironclad was the only one of the three Union ironclads that were any way near completion in early 1862, and it became inevitable that as soon as she was completed, the ironclad would be sent south to Hampton Roads. The vessel was launched on 30 January 1862, when she was named the USS *Monitor*, a name chosen by her designer and approved by Gideon Welles. Her crew of 49 men was completely unused to any such vessel, and they had to discover the quirks of their vessel during the voyage south to Hampton Roads. Although far smaller than the *Virginia*, the *Monitor* was capable of virtually all-round fire, and was protected by thicker armor. She was also far more maneuverable than her opponent, but she lacked the sheer weight of armament of her rival. Although some naval officers who viewed her claimed she could "sink any vessel afloat," others expected her to sink as soon as she was launched. The all-volunteer crews were brave men to venture to sea in such an untested experimental vessel, let alone take her into action against the most powerful warship in the Confederacy.

---

**USS *Monitor*'s Officers**
Commanding Officer: Lieutenant John Worden
Executive Officer: Lieutenant Samuel Dana Greene
Chief Engineering Officer: Lieutenant Stimers
Lieutenants (3), Midshipmen (5)
Surgeon: Daniel C. Logue
Paymaster: William Keeler

---

### The North Atlantic Blockading Squadron at Hampton Roads

The blockading squadron that lay in Hampton Roads during the first week of March 1862 was representative of the blockading forces that encircled the Confederacy. All were unarmored vessels, and almost all were wooden. The most powerful ships were the steam frigates USS *Minnesota* (Captain Gershon Van Brunt) and USS *Roanoke* (Captain John Marston), both well armed with the latest shell guns. Marston was also the acting commander of the squadron during the battle. The squadron also included several sailing warships, echoes of a bygone age. While they lacked the maneuverability of steam warships, they did possess a powerful enough armament, and were therefore useful, at least until more modern warships could be found to replace them. These sailing ships included the frigates USS *Congress* (Lieutenant Joseph Smith) and USS *St. Lawrence* (Captain H. Purvayance), plus the USS *Cumberland* (Captain William Radford), formerly a frigate that had been "razeed" or cut down to make a smaller but more useful warship. The squadron included myriad smaller ships, including transports, tugs to move the sailing vessels, supply ships, dispatch boats, small gunboats, a hospital ship, and a storeship. One oddity in the fleet was the *Vanderbilt*, a former iron paddlewheel steamer that had served as an ocean liner. She was due to be commissioned into the Navy, and was in Hampton Roads for the sole purpose of ramming the *Virginia* in the event of her appearance. As she had a top speed of 14 knots

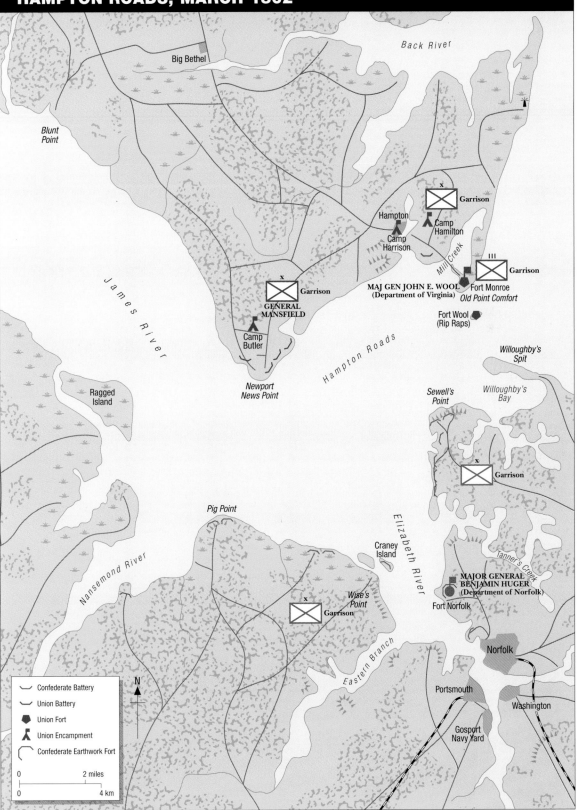

Back River

Big Bethel

Blunt
Point

Hampton

Camp
Hamilton

x  Garrison

Camp
Harrison

x  Garrison

Mill Creek

III  Garrison

MAJ GEN JOHN E. WOOL
(Department of Virginia)

Fort Monroe
Old Point Comfort

GENERAL
MANSFIELD

Fort Wool
(Rip Raps)

J a m e s   R i v e r

Camp
Butler

Newport
News Point

H a m p t o n   R o a d s

Willoughby's
Spit

Sewell's
Point

Willoughby's
Bay

Ragged
Island

x  Garrison

Pig Point

Craney
Island

E l i z a b e t h   R i v e r

Tanner's Creek

MAJOR GENERAL
BENJAMIN HUGER
(Department of Norfolk)

Fort Norfolk

N a n s e m o n d   R i v e r

x  Garrison

Wise's
Point

Norfolk

Eastern Branch

Washington

N

Portsmouth

Gosport
Navy Yard

### Legend

〜 Confederate Battery

〜 Union Battery

⬟ Union Fort

⚐ Union Encampment

◠ Confederate Earthwork Fort

0        2 miles

0        4 km

The USS *Minnesota* was the most powerful wooden warship in Hampton Roads during the battle. During the second day of the battle she was also the most vulnerable, having run aground the previous afternoon midway between Old Point Comfort and Newport News Point. Unable to free herself, she lay at the mercy of the *Virginia*. (National Archives)

and displaced over 3,000 tons, she might well have been successful if she had been given the opportunity to try. Anchored amongst the Union fleet as an impartial observer, the small French warship *Gassendi* was present under a flag of neutrality. Her commander, Captain Gautier, was charged with determining the effectiveness of the Confederate ironclad. He would find plenty to write about.

### The Union Defenses of Fort Monroe and Newport News
The northern shore of Hampton Roads was dominated by the imposing bulk of Fort Monroe, a brick-built fortification similar to other coastal fortifications that ringed the country from New England to the mouth of the Mississippi River. The fort was defended by 12,000 men, a total that included both its garrison and troops in outlying camps: Camp Butler at Newport News Point, Camp Hamilton two miles to the north, and Camp Harrison in the burned-out village of Hampton itself. The troops at Fort Butler were commanded by Brigadier General Joseph K. Mansfield, who also commanded the shore batteries lining Newport News Point. Halfway between Sewell's Point and Fort Monroe was a man-made island known as the "Rip Raps". A small round fortification

The sidewheel steamer *Vanderbilt* was a transatlantic liner that was donated to the US Navy as a free charter by the multimillionaire shipping tycoon Cornelius Vanderbilt. Plans were afoot to convert the liner into a giant ram to be used against the *Virginia*, but work had not yet started at the time of the battle. (US Navy)

had been built there, although work was far from complete. It was called Fort Wool, named after Major General John E. Wool, the commander of the Union Department of Virginia, whose headquarters was at Fort Monroe. Like their Confederate counterparts on the southern side of the Roads, these troops would have a grandstand view of the naval battle that would change the face of naval warfare.

## UNION VESSELS

**USS MONITOR** – Single-turret screw monitor (Armored)
**Built:** New York. **Commissioned:** February 1862
**Dimensions:** 179ft (length) x 41ft 6in. (beam) x 10ft 6in.
   (draft).
**Displacement:** 987 tons
**Armament:** 2 x 11in. smoothbores
**Armor:** 8in. turret and pilothouse, 4½in. hull, 1in. deck, all
   with timber backing.
**Complement:** 49
**Speed:** 8 knots

**USS CONGRESS** – Wooden Sailing Frigate (Unarmored)
**Built:** Portsmouth. **Commissioned:** May 1842
**Dimensions:** 179ft x 47ft 6in. x 22ft 6in.
**Displacement:** 1,867 tons
**Armament:** 10 x 8in. smoothbores, 40 x 30-pdr.
   smoothbores
**Complement:** 480

**USS CUMBERLAND** – Wooden Sailing Sloop*
   (Unarmored)
**Built:** Boston. **Commissioned:** November 1843
**Dimensions:** 175ft x 45ft x 22ft 4in.
**Displacement:** 990 tons
**Armament:** 22 x 9in. smoothbores, 1 x 10in.
   smoothbore, 1 x 170-pdr. rifle
**Complement:** 190
* Converted from a frigate in 1855

**USS MINNESOTA** – Wooden Screw Frigate (Unarmored)
**Built:** Washington. **Commissioned:** May 1857
**Dimensions:** 265ft x 51ft 4in. x 23ft 10in.
**Displacement:** 4,833 tons
**Armament:** 28 x 10in. smoothbores, 1 x 10in.
   smoothbore, 14 x 8in. smoothbores
**Complement:** 646
**Speed:** 12 knots

**USS ROANOKE** – Wooden Screw Frigate (Unarmored)
**Built:** Norfolk. **Commissioned:** May 1857
**Dimensions:** 268ft 6in. x 52ft 6in. x 23ft 9in.
**Armament:** 2 x 10in. smoothbores, 28 x 9in.
   smoothbores, 14 x 8in. smoothbores
**Complement:** 674
**Speed:** 11 knots

**USS VANDERBILT** – Wooden Sidewheel Gunboat
   (Unarmored)
**Built:** New York, 1856 (former merchant vessel).
**Acquired by Navy:** March 1862
**Dimensions:** 340ft x 47ft 6in. x 21ft 6in.
**Displacement:** 3,360 tons
**Armament:** None fitted by 8–9 March 1862
**Complement:** skeleton crew
**Speed:** 14 knots

**USS ST. LAWRENCE** – Wooden Sailing Frigate
   (Unarmored)
**Built:** Norfolk. **Commissioned:** September 1848
**Dimensions:** 175ft x 45ft x 22ft 4in.
**Displacement:** 1,726 tons
**Armament:** 10 x 8in. smoothbores, 30 x 32-pdr.
   smoothbores, 2 x 12-pdr. smoothbores
**Complement:** 400

**USS ZOUAVE** – Wooden Screw Tug (Unarmored)
**Built:** Albany, 1861 (former merchant vessel).
**Acquired by Navy:** December 1861
**Dimensions:** 95ft x 20ft 10in. x 9ft
**Armament:** 2 x 30-pdr. rifles
**Complement:** 25
**Speed:** 10 knots

**USS DRAGON** – Wooden Screw Tug (Unarmored)
**Built:** Buffalo, 1861 (former merchant vessel).
**Acquired by Navy:** December 1861
**Dimensions:** 92ft x 17ft x 9ft 6in.
**Armament:** 1 x 30-pdr. rifle, 1 x 24-pdr. smoothbore
**Complement:** 42
**Speed:** 8 knots

# BACKGROUND TO THE BATTLE

## WAR AND BLOCKADE

I n 1860, the United States of America lay on the brink of Civil War as North and South were drawn apart on issues of slavery and state rights. To all but the most hot-headed secessionist, war between the predominantly agrarian South and the largely industrialized North would lead to the overwhelming of the rebelling Southern states by sheer weight of manpower and material. The only chance for the Confederacy was a rapid military victory, ending the conflict before Northern industrial might could be brought to bear. On 20 December 1860, South Carolina elected to secede from the Union, and within weeks six other states followed her lead. On 4 February 1861, representatives of these states met in Montgomery, Alabama, and agreed to form a Confederacy. Four days later a provisional constitution was ratified, and this group of secessionist states officially became the Confederate States of America. Conflict with the North seemed inevitable, but for the next eight weeks America's fate hung in the balance. Next, the Confederate Congress elected a new President, Jefferson F. Davis of Mississippi, who was inaugurated on 18 February. Two days later, President Davis created the Confederacy's own Navy Department, naming Florida senator Stephen R. Mallory as its first chief.

Mallory faced a daunting challenge. The Confederate coastline would eventually stretch from the Potomac River to the Rio Grande, and while many Southern ports were protected by relatively modern brick-

The CSS *Virginia*, shown during her passage down the Elizabeth River on the morning of 8 August 1862. In the background is the naval hospital at Portsmouth where Flag Officer Buchanan was taken after the battle. The two ensigns shown are incorrect, and post-date the engagement. (US Navy)

This view of Hampton Roads shows Fort Monroe in the foreground, and Fort Wool (5), Sewell's Point (7), Craney Island (8), and the mouth of the Elizabeth River (9) in the background. Newport News Point (17) is on the right of the illustration. (Casemate)

built fortifications, Mallory had no navy to help defend this long coastline. The situation improved during March and early April, as hundreds of Southern naval officers resigned their commissions and returned home. Ships were commandeered and converted to form the nucleus of State navies, and Mallory worked on plans to create a dedicated naval force capable of protecting the Confederate coastline, although throughout the war he was plagued by shortages of men and resources. On 12 April 1861, Confederate guns opened fire on Fort Sumter, the bastion that protected the entrance to Charleston, South Carolina. President Lincoln called for volunteers to defend the Union, and proclaimed the institution of a blockade of the Confederate coastline. The war had begun.

To Secretary of the Navy Gideon Welles, Union naval strategy was deceptively simple. General Winfield Scott developed the "Anaconda Plan", whereby a tight naval blockade would cut off the Confederacy from the outside world. A major thrust down the Mississippi River would cut the country in two, allowing Union forces to squeeze the remaining parts of the Confederacy by land and naval attacks. Deprived of supplies and faced with the industrial might of the North, defeat would be inevitable. When the war began the US Navy was desperately short of ships capable of blockading Southern ports. Although the fleet consisted of over 90 ships, in April 1861, most were either being refitted and repaired in port, or were on deployment overseas. While the Navy launched a major shipbuilding program, Welles ordered the purchase and conversion of dozens of merchant vessels to help maintain the blockade until purpose-built warships became available. During the remainder of 1861, token Union naval squadrons appeared at the mouth of major Southern ports, such as Charleston, New Orleans, Mobile, Pensacola, Savannah, and Wilmington.

Minor naval clashes on the Potomac River ended when a blockading squadron appeared in Hampton Roads, effectively sealing off tidewater Virginia, including links between Richmond and Norfolk. The squadron was based off Fort Monroe, whose formidable defenses remained in

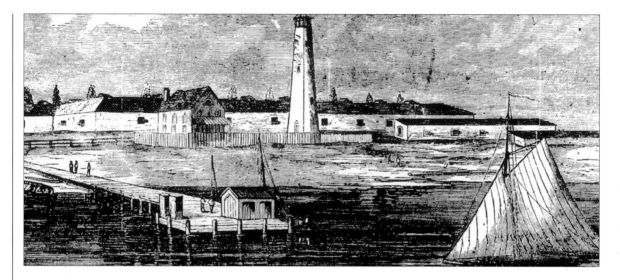

Union hands, and which served as a secure base in Virginia, across the bay from Norfolk. Combined naval and amphibious attacks secured the use of Hatteras Inlet in North Carolina's outer banks, and led to the capture of Port Royal, South Carolina. Both provided vital anchorages, as the only other secure Union anchorage south of Hampton Roads was Key West, off the southern tip of Florida. The Confederate capture of Norfolk ensured a sort of naval stalemate in Virginia's tidewater for another year. Although Union naval forces off Hampton Roads grew stronger during the winter and spring of 1862, and the strength of the Union garrison at Fort Monroe increased, neither side felt itself powerful enough to take offensive action. All that was to change with the conversion of the *Merrimac* into a powerful ironclad.

## THE CAPTURE OF NORFOLK NAVY YARD

In 1861, the steam frigate USS *Merrimac* was one of the most powerful warships in the US Navy. She was one of a series of six 40-gun steam frigates ordered in 1854, and from her launch in Boston the following year she was regarded as the pride of the fleet. She served in the West Indies and the Pacific before being sent to Norfolk Navy Yard in February 1860 for a major refit. Norfolk Navy Yard was considered the "premier yard" in the country. It covered 108 acres in the Gosport suburb of Portsmouth, across the Elizabeth River from Norfolk itself, and combined being a major shipbuilding yard with service as the Navy's primary ordnance and munitions depot. It boasted a large granite dry dock, machine shops, a foundry, and three shipbuilding slips. Work continued in the yard in early 1861 even though war seemed imminent, as the base commandant was reluctant to begin any evacuation, which might provoke Virginia to secede.

When Virginia withdrew from the Union on 17 April 1861 (five days after the bombardment of Fort Sumter), the base commander finally made plans to evacuate Norfolk and to destroy the facilities. He achieved little, partly as he was hindered by Southern sympathizers amongst his staff and civilian workforce, most of whom refused to carry

**The lighthouse on Old Point Comfort, with Fort Monroe behind it, viewed from the south. The jetty in the foreground was a hive of activity on 8 March, when the ironclad *Virginia* made her sortie into Hampton Roads, and the small vessels there fled behind the Point. (Casemate)**

OPPOSITE TOP **This emplacement to the northeast of Fort Monroe was sited to cover the passage between Fort Monroe and Fort Wool. Its primary function was to block the *Virginia*'s access to Chesapeake Bay. The 15in. Rodman smoothbore pictured here was nicknamed the "Lincoln Gun". (Casemate)**

OVERLEAF

**BUILDING THE CSS *VIRGINIA*, EARLY FEBRUARY, 1862.**
The CSS *Virginia* was converted from the burned-out remains of the wooden steam frigate USS *Merrimac*, with much of the work being carried out in the surviving dry dock in Norfolk Navy Yard. The scene is based on an engraving of the conversion process, which was later rendered as a painting. It depicts the final stages of the process, as the last iron plates are being bolted to the forward part of the *Virginia*'s casemate. This work was still being completed when the ship was commissioned into the Confederate Navy on 17 February, 1862. In the foreground, Flag Officer Franklin Buchanan is shown discussing the work with his second-in-command, Lieutenant Thomas Catesby ap Jones, while a junior Confederate naval officer waits behind Jones for his instructions. On the right of the scene the two figures shown in earnest discussion are John L. Porter, the Confederate Naval Constructor, and Commander John M. Brooke, CSN, the ordnance expert whose guns formed the vessel's main armament. (Adam Hook)

out his orders. On 20 April the commandant of the yard, Commodore Charles S. McCauley ordered the base destroyed and the *Merrimac* taken into the Elizabeth River, set on fire and scuttled, as he lacked the manpower to tow her to safety. Ironically a rescue party and a tug arrived from Fort Monroe to tow her away, but it was too late. If they had arrived earlier, the Battle of Hampton Roads would never have taken place. Of the 12 warships at the yard, only the sailing sloop USS *Cumberland* was towed to the safety of Fort Monroe, on the far side of Hampton Roads. Late the following evening the yard was abandoned, and the local Confederate militia marched in to claim their prize. Although an attempt had been made to destroy the dry dock, it was still serviceable, as were many of the shipyard facilities. Even more impressive was the haul of some 1,200 pieces of naval ordnance, including 300 modern Dahlgren smoothbores, 50 of them being his latest 11in. smoothbores. Within days, Confederate Secretary of the Navy Stephen Mallory visited the site, and work began hauling many of the guns away to arm coastal defenses in the Carolinas, Louisiana, and Georgia. Other pieces were hauled into place overlooking Hampton Roads to protect Norfolk itself. Two weeks later, scouting vessels dispatched from the north shore of Hampton Roads were turned back by fire from batteries on Sewell's Point and Pig Point. As trains brought up Confederate reinforcements from Richmond, General Wool at Fort Monroe deemed the Norfolk area too strong to be recaptured without a major and costly assault. Norfolk was safely in Confederate hands.

## CONVERTING THE *MERRIMAC*

During his visit, Mallory examined the wreck of the *Merrimac*. Across Hampton Roads, Flag Officer Silas Stringham, commander of the newly formed North Atlantic Blockading Squadron, deemed the wreck "worthless" in a letter to the Secretary of the Navy Gideon Welles. Mallory thought otherwise, and weeks after the fall of the Norfolk Navy Yard, he formed a design team, consisting of naval constructor John L. Porter, Lieutenant John M. Brooke and naval engineer William

P. Williamson. Mallory asked the men to sketch out plans for the conversion of the hulk into an armored warship, able to "prevent all blockade and encounter … their entire navy." His trio of designers was perfectly chosen. They inspected the *Merrimac*, ordered her salvage, and designed her rebirth as a revolutionary new warship. On 11 July they presented their proposals to Mallory, who was delighted and immediately gave the design his approval. He immediately wrote to Flag Officer French Forrest, the new Confederate commandant of the yard: "You will proceed with all practical dispatch to make changes in the *Merrimack* and to build, equip and fit her in all respects … you will see that work progresses without delay to completion." As the Battle of Bull Run ensured the survival of the Confederacy for another year, work began on the creation of the Confederate answer to the Union's naval blockade.

As early as 24 May the *Merrimac* was raised and hauled into Norfolk's dry dock. Mallory estimated that the work to convert the *Merrimac* would cost $172,523, a sizeable portion of his Department's allocated budget. He went ahead with the work without arguing for additional funding from the Confederate Congress, now housed in Richmond, Virginia. He understood that time was vital. Mallory commissioned the building of other casemate ironclads to protect the Mississippi River, but he realized the importance of the *Merrimac* project. The Union was also becoming uneasy, particularly when, on 17 October, Stringham's replacement Flag Officer Louis M. Goldsborough reported to Gideon Welles that: "I am now quite satisfied that … she will, in all probability, prove to be exceedingly formidable." News of the project had already caused the Union Navy Department to launch their own ironclad program, but it was increasingly becoming clear that both navies were locked in a race. If the Confederates were first to commission their ironclad, they could decimate the Union blockading squadron lying off Hampton Roads. Goldsborough sent regular reports, reporting in mid-October that the *Merrimac* was, "still in the dry dock at Norfolk, and yet needs a goodly quantity of iron to complete her casing, all of which is furnished from Richmond. She has her old engines on board, and they have been made to work tolerably well." He expected her to be ready by the start of November. This was an estimate that failed to take the Confederacy's

ABOVE **When the decision was made to abandon Norfolk Navy Yard, the USS *Cumberland* protected the base with her guns as Union sailors and soldiers destroyed ships that couldn't be removed to safety and ferried stores to Fort Monroe. (LoV)**

RIGHT **The destruction of the wooden steam frigate USS *Merrimac* at Washington Navy Yard, early in the morning of 19 April 1861. The vessel was burned to the waterline, but her lower hull and engines escaped serious damage, and were reused by the Confederate Navy. (Hensley)**

industrial and transport problems into account. The Tredegar Iron Works was reportedly "pressed beyond endurance" to fulfill the demands of the Navy Department. When plate was ready, it was sent by train from Richmond to Portsmouth via Petersburg, although the Army had priority, and trains carrying iron plates were frequently shunted into sidings or re-routed to allow troop or munitions trains to pass. Another problem was the shortage of railroad flatcars that could carry the weight of the metal plates. According to their records, the Tredegar Iron Works supplied 725 tons of armored plates for use on the *Merrimac*, for a total cost of $123,615. The majority of these were 10ft long, 8in. wide

The Norfolk Navy Yard was actually located in the southern suburb of Portsmouth known as Gosport. This photograph was taken after the virtual destruction of the base on 18–19 April 1861. The US Navy's failure to destroy the dry dock would have major repercussions. (LoV)

and 2in. thick, pre-drilled to allow them to be bolted to the wooden framework of the *Merrimac*'s casemate.

The sheer scale of the casemate was a challenge to Porter and his team of engineers. The structure was 172ft long, 30ft wide, and 7ft high. The rounded corners were a problem, as plate had to be curved, and the Tredegar works lacked the powerful hydraulic presses found in other yards. Work on these corners was, therefore, slow and laborious. Another problem was the production of a huge 1,500lb iron ram, which Porter wanted attached to the ironclad's bow, some 2ft below the waterline. The piece was duly produced, but neither Porter or the ironworkers knew how this ram would perform in combat. Ramming was a tactic used by galleys in the Mediterranean as late as the Renaissance, but the advent of reliable firepower at sea made the device redundant. Porter's "re-invention" of the ram demonstrated the extent to which he, Mallory, and other Confederate designers were leading a revolution in naval warfare.

The armament was supplied from two sources: the six 9in. Dahlgren's, which formed the bulk of the vessel's broadside armament, came from the stockpile of weapons captured when the Norfolk Navy Yard was captured. Some accounts claim they were the guns that were originally carried on the *Merrimac*, but there is no hard evidence to support this. Mallory was a strong advocate for the adoption of rifled ordnance. Under the guidance of Lieutenant Brooke, four rifled guns were cast at the Tredegar ironworks; two 6.4in. pieces, which would be fired as part of the main broadside, and two 7in. rifles, mounted at the bow and stern. The rifled guns were Brooke's own design, although they were for the most part improved versions of the Parrott guns used by the Union. The Confederates recognized the advantages of rifled guns, but although highly accurate, in practice their effectiveness was limited by problems with the supply of reliable projectiles and powder.

By the New Year of 1862, deserters reported to the Union that "the last of the iron plates for the *Merrimac* were put on". In fact, the ironclad was far from ready, as shortages of iron, guns, fittings, and almost all types of supplies delayed her construction. The ironclad was still weeks from completion, and although Flag Officer Buchanan arrived to oversee her completion, the ironclad was still short of a crew to man her.

## ERICSSON'S FOLLY

On 3 August 1861, the Union Navy Department secured Federal funding to build ironclads in response to the threat posed by the *Merrimac*. The "Ironclad Board" reviewed the 16 tenders that had been submitted, and encouraged by the financier Cornelius Bushnell, and prompted by Welles, the Board reluctantly approved the design proposed by John Ericsson. None of the board members were engineers, or even advocates of ironclad warships, but all three members understood the danger facing the blockading squadron in Hampton Roads. Of the two other tenders approved, the ironclad gunboat USS *Galena* would be commissioned in April 1862, and the powerful casemate ironclad USS *New Ironsides* would enter service four months later. As reports suggested the *Merrimac* would be ready for service by February at the latest, Ericsson's design for a turreted

When the Confederates captured Norfolk Navy Yard on the morning of 19 April 1861, they found 1,085 pieces of ordnance that had survived the destruction. These included modern Dahlgren smoothbores, which were subsequently mounted in the *Virginia*. (Hensley)

ironclad was the only vessel of the three that stood any chance of being commissioned in time to counter the *Merrimac*.

Ericsson was a designer of moderate means, and he lacked the capital needed to start work on the project. His alliance with the Connecticut financier Cornelius Bushnell ensured he had the support of Bushnell's friend Gideon Welles. It also brought Ericsson into contact with Bushnell's two partners, John Griswold and John Winslow, both of whom owned foundries on the Hudson River. It also ensured funds were available to undertake the project. On 27 September the four men signed a contract with the Navy and work began immediately.

The agreement signed by Ericsson and his three backers specified the vessel would be completed in just over four months. Sub-contracting much of the work helped speed the process, and the constituent parts would then be brought to the Continental Iron Works in Brooklyn for final assembly, under the supervision of Ericsson. The turret plates were to be manufactured in the Abbot foundry in Baltimore, while the hull plates came from John Winslow's own works in New York. Ericsson made all the design decisions; many of which involved compromises, such as the decision to use 1in. rather than 2in. plate for the turret, as the thicker metal would take too long to produce. The Novelty Iron Works of New York constructed the turret, as they had the most suitable hydraulic presses to bend the plate supplied by Abbot. Ericsson's friend Cornelius Delamater built the engines in his foundry in New York, while auxiliary engines were produced under contract in another foundry. As Ericsson boasted afterwards, production began even before the Navy Department clerks had drawn up the contract.

To many serving naval officers, the idea of a semi-submerged floating ironclad warship was preposterous, and they ridiculed the project in the press. Newspaper reporters dubbed the vessel "Ericsson's folly", and some contemporaries even doubted she would float. The initial contract specified the inclusion of "masts, spars, sails and rigging", a freeboard of 18in., and demanded that the vessel carry sufficient stores and water to

Camp Butler was sited close to Newport News Point, and served as a holding camp for troops garrisoning the tip of the Virginia Peninsula. Detachments of sharpshooters from the camp were used to provide supporting fire for the *Cumberland* and *Congress*. (LoV)

feed 100 men for three months. Clearly these were all devices added by the Navy to compromise the project, as was the clause whereby Ericsson and his backers remained liable for the vessel until the Navy approved its design. Twenty-five percent of the cost of the vessel was withheld by the Navy Department until the vessel's captain pronounced her a seaworthy and effective warship. This meant that when the *Monitor* steamed toward the *Virginia*, she was still partly owned by her builders!

The keel was laid on 25 October, and during the following month the project took shape. The lower hull was completed within three weeks, and work began on the raft-like upper hull. The turret was shipped to the Brooklyn yard in pieces, then assembled *in situ*. The engines were tested, then disassembled and installed before the vessel's deck beams were fitted. Ignoring the contract stipulations, the *Monitor*'s coal bunkers were sufficient for just over a week of steaming, which Ericsson considered sufficient for the needs of the vessel. By the first days of January, the vessel was nearing completion, and Ericsson informed the Navy Department that he wanted to call her the *Monitor*, so that "the ironclad … will thus prove a severe monitor" to the Confederacy. He added that "this last Yankee notion, this monitor" would also amaze the British. The name was approved, and on 30 January 1862 the *Monitor* was launched into the East River. Thousands had come to watch the launch, and many considered her the epitome of the "iron coffin" the vessel had been dubbed in the press. Confounding many of her critics, she floated. Ericsson's folly was almost ready for service, just four months after the Navy ordered her to be built. Ericsson ignored the contractual obligations to supply stores, masts, and other non-essentials, and instead he supplied the Navy with a revolutionary warship, custom built to fight Confederate ironclads.

Two weeks before the launch, the Navy Department named Lieutenant John Worden her first Commanding Officer, and Worden duly arrived at the Brooklyn Yard on 16 January. Worden was an experienced naval officer, and although a quiet, retiring man, one of his officers reckoned, "he will not hesitate to submit our iron sides to as severe a test as the most warlike could desire." As soon as the *Monitor* was launched he led his volunteer crew on board and together with Ericsson he examined his new command. He also supervised the installation of the two 11in. Dahlgren smoothbore guns into the *Monitor*'s turret. Despite pleas for larger 12in. Dahlgren pieces, the commandant at Brooklyn Navy Yard reported that none were available. It was the Navy's last attempt to prevent the ironclad's completion. Like many other features about the *Monitor*, her armament was a compromise, as Worden and Ericsson settled for 11in. guns instead. Worden formally took command of the ironclad at 2.00pm on 19 February 1862, and although an initial trial demonstrated problems with her engines, the vessel was duly commissioned into the Navy six days later. The USS *Monitor* was ready for active service.

## THE LONG VOYAGE SOUTH

John Ericsson never claimed that the USS *Monitor* was an ocean-going vessel. Instead, it was designed for use in shallow coastal waters such as Hampton Roads. Lieutenant Worden completed his provisioning of the *Monitor* in Brooklyn Navy Yard, and on 4 March he received his orders to take her to Hampton Roads. The Atlantic seaboard was in the grip of a severe storm, so Worden delayed his departure for two days, waiting for the storm to subside. At 11.00am on 6 March he secured a towline from the screw tug *Seth Low*, and was led out of New York harbor. The tug was there to augment the small engines of the *Monitor*, and to be ready to help in the event of any mishap. The wooden screw gunboats USS *Sachem* and USS *Currituck* provided an armed escort.

By the end of the afternoon watch (4.00pm), the flotilla rounded Sandy Hook and turned south to follow the New Jersey coast. The

The incomplete walls of Fort Wool were built on the Rip Raps shoal, halfway between Old Point Comfort and Willoughby's Spit. It, therefore, helped seal off the entrance into Hampton Roads from Chesapeake Bay. (Casemate)

# THE *MONITOR*'S VOYAGE TO HAMPTON ROADS, 6–9 MARCH 1862

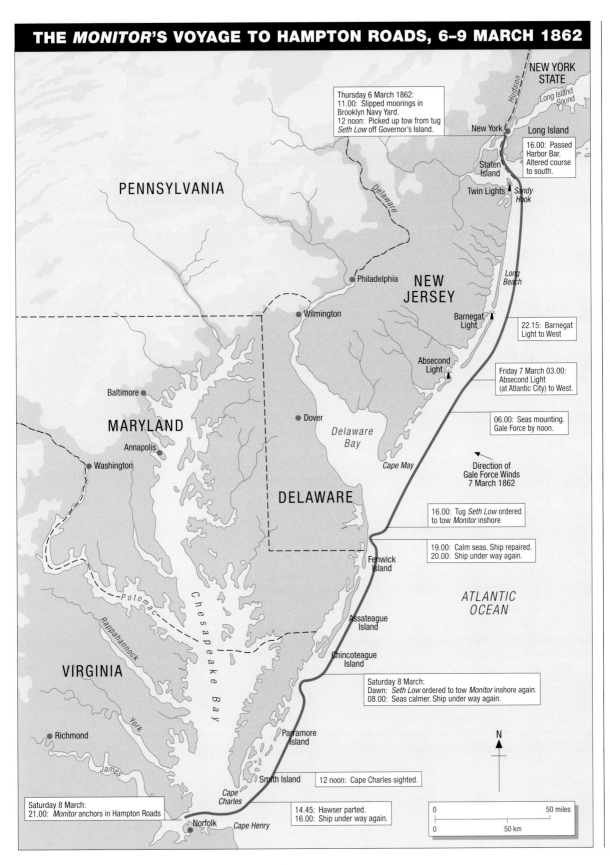

NEW YORK STATE

Long Island Sound

Hudson

**Thursday 6 March 1862:**
11.00: Slipped moorings in Brooklyn Navy Yard.
12 noon: Picked up tow from tug *Seth Low* off Governor's Island.

New York

Long Island

**16.00: Passed Harbor Bar. Altered course to south.**

Staten Island

PENNSYLVANIA

Delaware

Twin Lights — Sandy Hook

Philadelphia

NEW JERSEY

Long Beach

Wilmington

Barnegat Light

**22.15: Barnegat Light to West**

Baltimore

MARYLAND

Dover

Absecond Light

**Friday 7 March 03.00: Absecond Light (at Atlantic City) to West.**

Annapolis

Delaware Bay

**06.00: Seas mounting. Gale Force by noon.**

Washington

Cape May

Direction of Gale Force Winds 7 March 1862

DELAWARE

**16.00: Tug *Seth Low* ordered to tow *Monitor* inshore**

**19.00: Calm seas. Ship repaired.
20.00: Ship under way again.**

Fenwick Island

ATLANTIC OCEAN

Potomac

Chesapeake Bay

Assateague Island

Rappahannock

Chincoteague Island

VIRGINIA

**Saturday 8 March:**
Dawn: *Seth Low* ordered to tow *Monitor* inshore again.
08.00: Seas calmer. Ship under way again.

York

Parramore Island

N

Richmond

James

Smith Island

**12 noon: Cape Charles sighted.**

Cape Charles

**Saturday 8 March:**
**21.00: *Monitor* anchors in Hampton Roads**

**14.45: Hawser parted.
16.00: Ship under way again.**

Norfolk

Cape Henry

| 0 | | 50 miles |
|---|---|---|
| 0 | | 50 km |

Brigadier General Joseph K. F. Mansfield (center figure) commanded the Union forces at Camp Butler and Newport News Point during the battle. His attempts to prevent the Confederates reaching the *Congress* after she had surrendered led to the destruction of the vessel. (Hensley)

*Monitor* continued on throughout the night, and sea conditions were relatively calm. The Navy Department's Chief Engineer, Alban Stimers, was attached to the ship to see how she performed. He recorded that despite the lack of swell, "as soon as we were outside of Sandy Hook the sea washed over the deck so deeply that it was not considered safe to permit the men to go on deck." Whatever the conditions, they seem to have deteriorated during the night. By 10.15pm Barnegat Light on Long Beach was due west, and the log recorded "fine weather." Seven hours later it reported it was "cold and clear," and the flotilla was six miles to seaward of the Absecond Light at Atlantic City. This meant the *Monitor* made an average speed of 5 knots throughout the night. By dawn conditions had worsened. A light gale had reappeared from the west, and at 6.00am the log recorded "very heavy sea. Ship making heavy weather." Worden was suffering from severe sea sickness, and moved to the top of the turret to revive himself. By mid-morning it was clear the *Monitor* had been caught in a full gale, and water broke over the turret. It even slammed through the vision slit in the pilothouse with such force that the helmsman was knocked over. The ship started leaking from the base of the turret. It had been designed to rest on a brass ring when not in use, and Ericsson argued that the weight of the turret provided an adequate seal. Worden had ignored Ericsson's advice, and had raised the turret, caulked the ring with oakum and lowered it again. The oakum had washed away, and water poured through "like a waterfall". Seawater also poured down into the engine room through ventilation ducts, soaking the leather belts that turned the engine fans. They were designed to remove poisonous fumes, and the water stopped them working. Within an hour the engine room was filled with carbon dioxide and carbonic gas. During the afternoon the engineers struggled to restart the blowers, but the fumes forced them to abandon the attempt. Chief Engineer Isaac Newton ordered the engine room abandoned, but the fumes quickly spread throughout the ship. Half-sinking and filled with poisonous gases, the *Monitor* was in danger of foundering, and Worden signaled for help. The *Seth Low* towed her into the shore, and in calmer waters, the engineers managed to vent the engine room and restart their machinery, including the pumps. Disaster had been averted.

The launch of the USS *Monitor* on 30 January 1862 was witnessed by thousands of spectators, many of whom were convinced the ironclad would never float. This contemporary lithograph is incorrect, as her turret was fitted after she was launched. (US Navy)

By 8.00pm on Friday 7 March, the *Monitor* was ready to resume her journey. The gale had passed on to the north and sea conditions were moderate as she steamed southwards past Fenwick Island. Lieutenant Greene reported a "smooth sea, clear sky, the moon out, and the old tank going along five and six knots very nicely." Around midnight they passed Chincoteague Island on the Maryland coast, but soon afterwards the swell increased. Water passed through the hawsepipe, making a "dismal, awful sound", and Worden ordered the hawsepipe stopped up to prevent any leaks. The seas started breaking over the smokestacks and ventilation ducts again. For the next few hours it remained doubtful whether the engines could continue, but somehow they kept turning. At one point the tiller ropes came loose, and the vessel turned "broadside to the seas and rolling over and over in all kinds of ways." It seemed likely the *Monitor* would be capsized if struck by a rogue wave, but within half an hour the wheel was working again. By dawn the seas had abated slightly, allowing Worden to signal the *Seth Low* to tow her inshore again. By 8.00am the *Monitor* and her escorts were in sheltered coastal waters again, and the crew ate breakfast. They had come close to disaster twice, but the ironclad remained afloat and her engines still worked. She was pumped dry and the voyage south continued.

At noon the quartermaster recorded "fine weather and clear sky." The worst was behind them, and Worden sighted Cape Charles, marking the northern entrance to Chesapeake Bay. The *Monitor* was on the last leg of her epic maiden voyage. At 2.45pm the *Seth Low's* towing hawser parted, but this was quickly replaced and the flotilla resumed its progress. A few minutes later Cape Henry Light became visible, and further to the right smoke lingered over Hampton Roads. Lieutenant Keeler recorded "as we approached still nearer little black spots could occasionally be seen." These were shells bursting in the air. Worden assumed the worst. Unable to steam any faster, he prepared his ship for action. When a pilot boat came out to meet the *Monitor*, the Pilot confirmed their fears. The *Merrimac* was destroying the blockading squadron. It was 9.00pm when Worden finally dropped anchor in Hampton Roads alongside the flagship USS *Roanoke*. He immediately sent a message to Washington announcing his safe arrival. Captain and crew then prepared themselves for the battle that would almost certainly take place the following morning.

## BUCHANAN TAKES COMMAND

On or around 14 February the *Merrimac* was relaunched, and on 16 February 1862 the Navy officially acquired the *Merrimac*, which was duly, renamed the CSS *Virginia*. There was no ceremony, and one sailor recorded "only four marines and a corporal were on board at her launching." A week later Flag Officer Franklin Buchanan arrived in Norfolk to oversee the completion of the ironclad. "Old Buck" and his staff found her far from ready for action, particularly as the vessel was still short of crewmen. While the Executive Officer, Lieutenant Smith, supervised the last-minute preparations of the *Virginia*, Buchanan sent Lieutenant John Wood, the grandson of President Zachary Taylor, to ask the Army for help. Wood met General Magruder near Yorktown, and of the 200 men who volunteered, the naval officer selected 80 artillerymen or former seamen to serve on board the *Virginia*. Jones was a hard taskmaster, and he hounded the construction crew and dockyard staff, while complaining to Buchanan about "the want of skilled labor and

The USS *Monitor* as she looked when she was commissioned. Following the battle, improvements were made to her pilot house and to her smokestacks (funnels), which were too low to prevent seawater from pouring into the boilers. (Hensley)

lack of proper tools and appliances." Everything in the wartime Confederacy was in short supply, and constant delays in the delivery of iron, coal, ammunition, powder, caulking, ropes, and lubricating oil kept Jones fully occupied. At one stage he even sent a naval party up the railroad track toward Petersburg to locate a missing shipment of iron.

While these preparations continued, Buchanan considered how best to use the ironclad. She drew 22ft of water, and the waters of the Elizabeth River and Hampton Roads were a maze of shallows and narrow channels. She was going to be difficult to turn, and given the constricted waters between Norfolk and Newport News Point, Buchanan was severely limited as to where he could steam. Even with a good local pilot, he would be unable to get close to either Fort Monroe or Newport News, and a large patch of shallows between Sewell's Point and Pig Point limited her area of operations even further. It was unlikely that the *Virginia* could sail far up the James River toward Richmond, but at least she could attack the larger vessels of the blockading squadron, forcing them to flee or run aground to avoid destruction.

On 4 March, Buchanan wrote to Mallory from "aboard the C.S. Steam Frigate *Virginia*." He acknowledged receipt of his appointment as Flag Officer commanding "the Naval Defenses of the James River," and he reported that "today I hoisted my flag aboard this ship." He went on to outline his plan of operation. "On Thursday night the 6th instant, I contemplate leaving here to appear before the Enemy's Ships at Newport News. Should no accident occur to this ship, when I feel confident that the acts of the *Virginia* will give proof of the desire of her officers and crew to meet the views of the Department as far as practicable." Buchanan was referring to Mallory's stated aim to use the ironclad to break the Union blockade of the Chesapeake. He added: "From the best and most reliable information I can obtain from experienced pilots it will be impossible to ascend the Potomac in the *Virginia* with the present draft of water, nearly 22 feet." He was gently letting Mallory know that his pipe dream of using the *Virginia* to bombard Washington was exactly that.

Buchanan wrote to Commander Tucker of the "James River Squadron," asking him to stand by to assist his attack. Jones counseled a delay. None of the gunport shutters had been fitted, and powder and shot had only just arrived. The attack was delayed for a day, allowing Jones to grease the casemate sides to "increase the tendency of projectiles to glance," and to rig temporary gunport shutters at the bow and stern. All the crew went on board on Thursday 6 March, and in Jones' words, "all preparations were made." Pilots were consulted, and a further postponement was recommended, as navigation of the Elizabeth River would be easier. The *Virginia's* sortie against the enemy fleet would take place at dawn on Saturday 8 March 1862.

# THE BATTLE OF HAMPTON ROADS

## "BLACK SMOKE IN THE ELIZABETH RIVER"
### The Sortie of the CSS *Virginia*, Saturday 8 March 1862

Flag Officer Buchanan's plan to attack the Union blockading fleet in Hampton Roads on Thursday 6 March was cancelled. The CSS *Virginia* was still not ready for action, and Lieutenant Jones begged for a few more days to finish preparing the ironclad. Buchanan had planned a night attack, but local pilots refused to take responsibility for guiding the ship up the Elizabeth River in the dark. The attack was postponed until Saturday morning. Even then, the gunport shields would still not be fitted, and finishing work on the warship such as the construction of internal compartments had to wait until after her maiden voyage. Lieutenant Wood recorded that prior to her sailing into action, "not a gun had been fired, hardly a revolution of her engines had been made." The ugly, ungainly *Virginia* would have to go into battle without the luxury of being fully completed, or even having run sea trials to test her performance. Neither her officers nor men knew what to expect. As the ironclad prepared for action, Buchanan claimed that she was only going to

The tug *Seth Low* towed the USS *Monitor* out of the Brooklyn Navy Yard, and then escorted her during the ironclad's eventful voyage south to Hampton Roads. On two occasions the tug had to tow the *Monitor* inshore to prevent her from being swamped. (US Army Military History Institute)

Sailors manning the hand-operated pumps inside the USS *Monitor*. During her voyage from New York to Hampton Roads the ironclad was almost swamped in heavy seas. Nine months later she foundered off Cape Hatteras in similar conditions. (Author's Collection)

perform trials on the Elizabeth River. Nobody seemed fooled by this, and the local press and public were well aware that the ironclad would sail into action against the enemy on Saturday morning. Buchanan briefed the commander of the James River Squadron, and requested that the three gunboats be ready to cooperate with him on Saturday morning. Apart from the ironclad itself, everything else was ready for the coming battle.

Lieutenant Jones later wrote of her condition before she went into action. "The lower part of her shield forward was only immersed a few inches instead of two feet as intended, and there was but one inch of iron on the (lower) hull. The port-shutters, etc. were unfinished. The *Virginia* was unseaworthy; her engines were unreliable, and her draft, over 22 feet, prevented her from going to Washington …" The surgeon Dinwiddie Phillips wrote that "many of those who watched us predicted failure." A naval friend of H. Ashton Ramsay, the *Virginia*'s Chief Engineer took the opportunity to tease his colleague, exclaiming "Goodbye Ramsay. I shall never see you again. She will prove your coffin." Many others probably shared these sentiments. Ramsay claimed there was an air of desperation in Flag Officer Buchanan as he ordered the workmen to leave the ship, and prepared the ironclad for her

The USS *Monitor* in heavy seas. Given her low freeboard, even a gentle swell could be enough to cause the ironclad to founder. Watercolor by Clary Roy, c.1900. (US Navy)

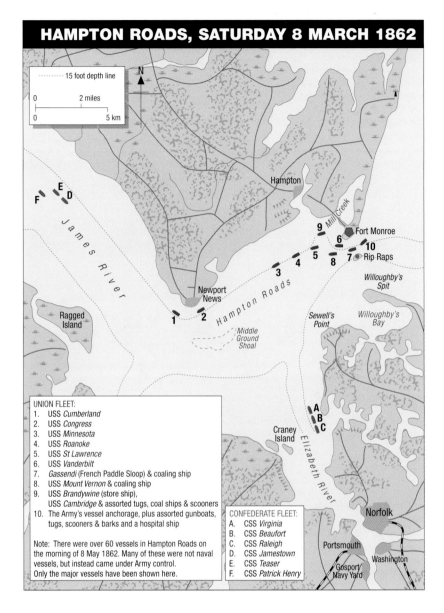

**HAMPTON ROADS, SATURDAY 8 MARCH 1862**

------- 15 foot depth line

0       2 miles
0       5 km

UNION FLEET:
1. USS *Cumberland*
2. USS *Congress*
3. USS *Minnesota*
4. USS *Roanoke*
5. USS *St Lawrence*
6. USS *Vanderbilt*
7. *Gassendi* (French Paddle Sloop) & coaling ship
8. USS *Mount Vernon* & coaling ship
9. USS *Brandywine* (store ship),
   USS *Cambridge* & assorted tugs, coal ships & scooners
10. The Army's vessel anchorage, plus assorted gunboats,
    tugs, scooners & barks and a hospital ship

Note: There were over 60 vessels in Hampton Roads on
the morning of 8 May 1862. Many of these were not naval
vessels, but instead came under Army control.
Only the major vessels have been shown here.

CONFEDERATE FLEET:
A. CSS *Virginia*
B. CSS *Beaufort*
C. CSS *Raleigh*
D. CSS *Jamestown*
E. CSS *Teaser*
F. CSS *Patrick Henry*

journey down the river. The tug CSS *Beaufort* (commanded by
Lieutenant William H. Parker, CSN) nudged the ironclad away from the
dock, and the *Virginia* slowly moved into the river channel, the Beaufort
following like a protective hen. It was 11.00am.

It was ten miles from the wharf in Gosport to Hampton Roads. The
ironclad had a top speed of about five or six knots, but made seven with
the river current. It would be at least 1½ hours before she would engage
the enemy, giving ample time for the entire garrison and population of
Norfolk and its hinterland to watch her journey down the Elizabeth
River. While Flag Officer Buchanan paced the upper spar deck of the
*Virginia*, thousands of onlookers crowded the banks and waved at him.
One crewman also noted that some "seemed too deeply moved by the
gravity of the moment to break into cheers." Small boats jostled for
position as the *Beaufort* and *Virginia* steamed past them, but "no voice
broke the silence of the scene; all hearts were too full for utterance. All

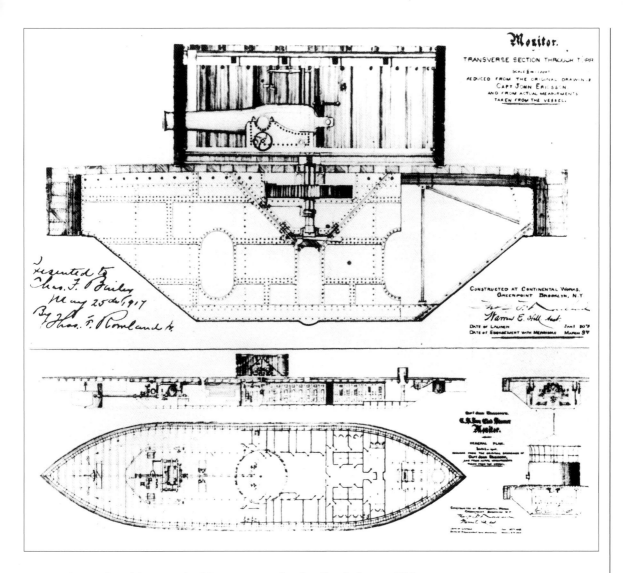

A cross-section through the turret of the USS *Monitor*, showing her guns run forward into their firing position. Thomas Rowland of the Continental Iron Works presented the plan to the Mariners Museum. (Mariners)

present knew that this was a decisive moment for the Confederacy. If the *Virginia* broke the enemy blockade, then there was a significant chance that the nation would gain the recognition and support of foreign powers such as Britain and France. With their support, the survival of the Confederacy was far more likely. William F. Drake, an artilleryman who had volunteered to crew one of the guns knew "ten thousand waving handkerchiefs told us that in their hearts they were bidding us Godspeed!" A local journalist was more eloquent. "It was a gallant sight to see the ironclad leviathan gliding noiselessly through the water flying the red pennant of her commander at the fore flag staff and the gay Confederate ensign aft…" To the inexperienced eye, all was going smoothly. In fact, the *Virginia's* steering mechanism was proving to be highly erratic, and two miles below Norfolk, Jones hailed the *Beaufort* and requested a tow. The ironclad would continue down the river under tow from the tugboat. A second armed tugboat, the CSS *Raleigh* was also called to help keep the *Virginia's* bows pointed down river.

It was at this stage that Buchanan stopped pacing and questioned Ramsay, his engineer. He asked him: "what would happen to your

An artist's rendition of the interior of the USS *Monitor*, drawn after the battle. Although inaccurate, it presents an atmospheric impression of the scene inside her pilot house and her turret. (Author's Collection)

engines and boilers if there should be a collision?" Ramsay replied that they would take the shock of impact. Buchanan then turned and addressed his senior officers. "I am going to ram the *Cumberland*. I am told she has the new rifled guns, the only ones in their whole fleet we have cause to fear. The moment we are in the roads, I'm going to make right for her and ram her." The decision had been made. The hands were piped to dinner, and the crew prepared themselves for battle. Ramsay went to join the other officers behind the curtained-off wardroom, but he passed the assistant surgeon laying out his instruments. "The sight took away my appetite," he recalled.

By noon, the *Virginia* and her consorts had drawn level with Sewell's Point, guarding the mouth of the Elizabeth River. For the first time, the crew could make out the enemy ships on the northern shore of Hampton Roads. Ramsay remembered seeing: "*Congress* and *Cumberland*, tall and stately, with every line and spar clearly defined against the blue March sky." The journalist from the *Norfolk Day Book* described his first view of the two Union ships "rising like prodigious castles over the placid water." The rigging of the USS *Cumberland* was covered with sailors' clothing hung out to dry, giving the ship a somewhat festive appearance. It looked as if the *Virginia*'s sortie had taken the Union fleet by surprise.

There were over 60 Union vessels in Hampton Roads that morning; warships, transports, supply ships, tugs, dispatch vessels, and tenders. Most of the vessels were powered by sail, and all lacked any form of armored protection. While many were naval vessels (or at least operated by the Navy), others came under the control of the Army Quartermaster Corps. Even the warships included a strange assortment of vessels, from powerful wooden steam frigates to former New York ferry boats that had been hastily converted into gunboats. The flagship of the Hampton Roads squadron was the USS *Minnesota*, an unarmored wooden steam-powered frigate mounting 43 large smoothbore guns. Rear-Admiral Louis M. Goldsborough was away at Hatteras Inlet, so Captain John Marston, the commander of the USS *Roanoke* was the senior Union naval officer in Hampton Roads that morning. The *Roanoke* was another

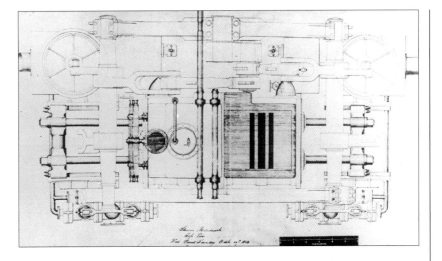

unarmored steam-powered frigate, but her engines were in the process of being overhauled, and her screw (propeller) shaft had been sent to Brooklyn Navy Yard. In order to join in any fight, she would have to use her sails, or else be towed into action. She carried 44 smoothbore guns. Captain Van Brunt commanded the *Minnesota*. She was anchored next to the *Vanderbilt*, one of the oddest ships in the squadron.

As a countermeasure against the *Virginia* the 5,000-ton transatlantic steamship had been recently chartered by the Navy. It was intended to plate her sides with iron, and to reinforce her bow with timber. If the *Virginia* appeared, the *Vanderbilt* would be used to ram her. The unarmed paddlewheel liner was still waiting for the work parties to begin her conversion when the *Virginia* sortied from the Elizabeth River. Anchored close to her was the USS *St. Lawrence*, a wooden sailing frigate that carried 42 guns of various sizes. All three of these warships lay off Fort Monroe, to the northeast of the mouth of the Elizabeth River.

Two more sailing warships lay to the northwest, off Newport News Point. The USS *Congress* was a wooden sailing frigate that carried 50 smoothbore guns. She was short of crew to man her, and although her full complement was 480 men, she was short of 80 men that morning, and even then her crew included a detachment of 89 soldiers from the 99th New York Infantry. She also had two captains. Commander W.B. Smith had just handed his ship over to Lieutenant Joseph B. Smith, but the Commander remained on board, waiting for a passage to take him to his new appointment. The Paymaster of the *Congress* was McKean Buchanan, the brother of the Confederate commander. Neither sibling knew that the other was on board either the *Virginia* or the *Congress*. Further to the west lay the wooden sailing sloop USS *Cumberland*, commanded by Captain William Radford. That morning he was away from his ship, as he was taking part in a court-martial on board the USS *Roanoke*. This meant his Executive Officer, Lieutenant George U. Morris was left in command. The *Cumberland* started her career as a sailing frigate, a sister ship of the *St. Lawrence*. Commissioned in 1845, she was "razeed" ten years later. This involved having her upper deck removed, making her a lower, lighter vessel. She was reclassified as a sloop. In March 1861 she carried 24 guns, including one rifled gun, mounted in her stern.

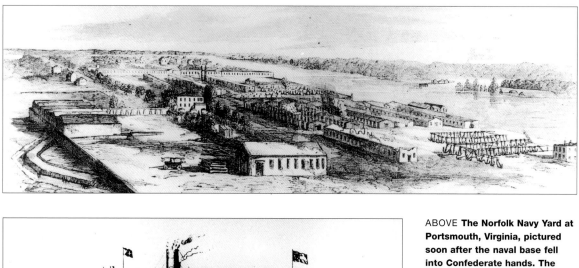

PROW, OF STEEL.
WOODEN BULWARK.
PILOT-HOUSE.

THE "MERRIMAC," FROM A SKETCH MADE THE DAY BEFORE THE FIGHT.

*Lt. R. L. Blackford, del. March 7, 1862*
*d d* IRON UNDER WATER
*f* PROPELLER.

ABOVE **The Norfolk Navy Yard at Portsmouth, Virginia, pictured soon after the naval base fell into Confederate hands. The lithograph omits to show the numerous vessels that were burned and scuttled in the Elizabeth River (to the right of the picture). These included the USS *Merrimac*. (LoV)**

LEFT **The CSS *Virginia* as she appeared just before the battle. During the first day of the battle she flew the Confederate ensign from her stern, and a blue Flag Officer's pennant from her forward staff. The latter flag was taken down when Flag Officer Buchanan was taken ashore. (Hensley)**

The tugboat *Zouave* (commanded by Acting Master Henry Reaney) began her career towing grain barges on the upper Hudson River. Now she was berthed at the dock at Newport News, where she acted as the tug and guard vessel for the two sailing warships off the Point. Sources contradict each other, but two army transport vessels were probably moored to the same wharf. Of the remainder of the shipping in Hampton Roads, most were clustered around Fort Monroe, either on the eastern, Chesapeake Bay side of Point Comfort, or off her southwest side. Other vessels lay further inshore, closer to the burned remains of the village of Hampton. These ships included the store ship *Brandywine*, a sister ship of the *St. Lawrence* and the *Cumberland*.

Anchored between Fort Monroe and Fort Wool was the small French paddlewheel gunboat *Gassendi*, commanded by Captain Ange Simon Gautier. She was there to observe any clash between the blockading squadron and the *Virginia*, and report the outcome to the French government. A group of her officers had just returned from a visit to Norfolk under a flag of truce. As neutral observers, the French naval officers were allowed to see the *Virginia*, but kept their observations to themselves. They were there as impartial observers, and over the next two days they were presented with a spectacle that her Captain would find "très intéressante."

The *Gassendi* provided the Union Navy with the first indication that something was about to happen. Around 10.00am she began taking on coal, an indication that she planned to shift her anchorage. Protocol demanded that she inform the Union flagship of any plan to depart, so that both nations could exchange the correct salutes. No such notification had been made. As the staff in Fort Monroe were well aware

The powerful wooden steam frigate USS *Merrimac* pictured entering Southampton Harbour during a courtesy visit to Britain in September 1856. In her day she was the most powerful and up-to-date vessel in the US Navy. (Mariners)

that the French had visited Norfolk the previous day, they suspected the French knew something, and planned to get out of the line of fire of the Fort. The Fort's commander, Major General John E. Wool, sent a telegram to Brigadier General Joseph K. Mansfield, commanding the Union troops encamped near Newport News Point. It asked him to keep a sharp lookout. Mansfield duly ordered the gun batteries lining the point to be manned and ready. Despite the warning, there was little other activity among the Union ships and men in the area. Many believed that the *Virginia* was far from ready, and there was little chance of action that morning. Soon after 11.00am, the signalers manning Mansfield's lookout station on Newport News Point reported seeing smoke rising far up the Elizabeth River. There was some form of Confederate naval activity going on, and Mansfield sent a telegram to Wool, claiming that "the *Merrimack* is close at hand." Apparently, neither General saw fit to share their suspicions with their naval colleagues. When the *Virginia* appeared off Sewell's Point, the Union blockading squadron was caught completely unprepared. The washing hanging from the rigging of the *Cumberland* was ample evidence of the fleet's lack of readiness.

To Lieutenant Tom Selfridge of the *Cumberland*, the early spring morning was "mild, bright and clear." With hardly any wind to ruffle the glassy surface of Hampton Roads, it promised to be a beautiful day. This all changed at about 12.45pm, when Henry Reaney on the *Zouave* noticed "black smoke in the Elizabeth River." He cast off and steamed alongside the *Cumberland*, where Selfridge was the officer of the deck. He had also spotted the smoke, and ordered Reaney to investigate. Within minutes the *Zouave* was heading south toward Pig Point, on the southern shore of the Roads. Reaney later reported: "It did not take us long to find out, for we had not gone over two miles when we saw what to all appearances looked like the roof of a very large barn belching forth smoke as from a chimney fire." The *Zouave* fired her 30-pdr. Parrot

rifle six times, then spun around and headed back towards the relative safety of Newport News. The time was 1.20pm. Reaney had fired the opening shots in the Battle of Hampton Roads. At the same time as Selfridge and Reaney spotted the *Virginia*, lookouts elsewhere in the squadron spotted the enemy warships. The logbook of the *Minnesota* that morning recorded that: "at 12.45pm saw three steamers off Sewell's Point standing towards Newport News; one of these was supposed to be the *Merrimack* from the size of her smokestack. We immediately slipped chain with buoy and rope attached at the 15-fathom shackle and steamed towards Newport News." Signals alerted the rest of the fleet, and the alarm drum call alerted the garrisons of Fort Monroe and Camp Butler. The French Captain Gautier shared Reaney's views concerning the appearance of the *Virginia*, which he described as "a barracks room surmounted by a large funnel." On board the Confederate ironclad, Chief Engineer Ramsay recorded the effect the *Virginia* had on the shipping in Hampton Roads. "The white-winged sailing craft that sprinkled the bay and long lines of tugs and boats scurried to the far shore like chickens on the approach of a hovering hawk." The *Minnesota* was seen to raise steam, and the clotheslines on the *Cumberland* were ripped down. Sails were raised on the *Congress*. The combatants on both sides prepared for battle.

**"All was lost except honor**." **The destruction of the *Cumberland***
Before he led the *Virginia* into action, Flag Officer Buchanan addressed his crew. "Sailors, in a few minutes you will have the long-looked-for opportunity of showing your devotion to our cause. Remember that you are about to strike for your country and your homes. The Confederacy expects every man to do his duty. Beat to Quarters!" The crew went to their stations, and one would note that: "the strictest discipline was in force on our gun deck, no one at the guns was allowed to talk, not even in a whisper. Everything was ready, guns loaded, and run out for action…." On the *Congress*, Captain Smith made a less Nelsonian speech.

Representation of the gun crews in action on board the CSS *Virginia*. Although the gun ports are too large and the wrong shape, the details of the guns, carriages and crew are accurate. The guns shown are her 9in. Dahlgren smoothbores, part of her broadside armament. (Hensley)

"My hearties, you see before you the great southern bugaboo, got up to frighten us out of our wits. Stand to your guns, and let me assure you that one good broadside from our gallant frigate and she is ours!" A similar silence then descended on the *Congress* as her crew watched the *Virginia* approach. Further to the east, the *Minnesota* was steaming toward Newport News, while the tugs *Dragon* and *Young America* were preparing to tow the *Roanoke* into action. The gunboat USS *Cambridge* already had the *St. Lawrence* under tow. An observer on the gunboat USS *Mystic* described it as "a sorry fleet to attack a vessel like the *Merrimack*...." The *Virginia* veered a little to starboard, then to port, as she tested her steering. She then headed straight for the *Congress*.

At around 2.00pm, the *Beaufort* fired the first Confederate shot of the day at the *Congress*. She was steaming on the port beam of the *Virginia*, and the shot was in response to Buchanan's signal, ordering "Close Action." The shot fell short. The fragile little armed tug stayed in the middle of Hampton Roads, as closing any further with the *Congress* would be suicidal. The *Virginia* steamed on alone. A few miles to the east, the wooden Union warships making their way toward Newport News came under fire from Sewell's Point soon after 2.00pm. One shot hit the *Minnesota's* mainmast, and she returned the fire while repairs were made. The other Union warships altered course to stay out of range.

The *Congress* held her fire until her gunners could make out the ports and armored plates on the casemate of the *Virginia* (around 500 yards). She then "tried her with a solid shot from one of our stern guns, the projectile glancing off her forward casemate like a drop of water from a duck's back...." At approximately 2.20pm the *Virginia* replied by firing a round of grapeshot from her forward gun, which killed or wounded about a dozen sailors on board the frigate. Next, with "a tremendous roar," the *Congress* fired her full broadside of 25 guns, including five 8in. Dahlgren smoothbores. Watching from the shore, Private Josh Lewis of the 20th Indiana Regiment recalled that the broadside "rattled on the armored *Merrimack* without the least injury."

The CSS *Virginia* managed to rake the stern of the stranded wooden frigate USS *Congress* from a range of less than 200 yards. Her fire turned the frigate into a "charnel house". (VWM)

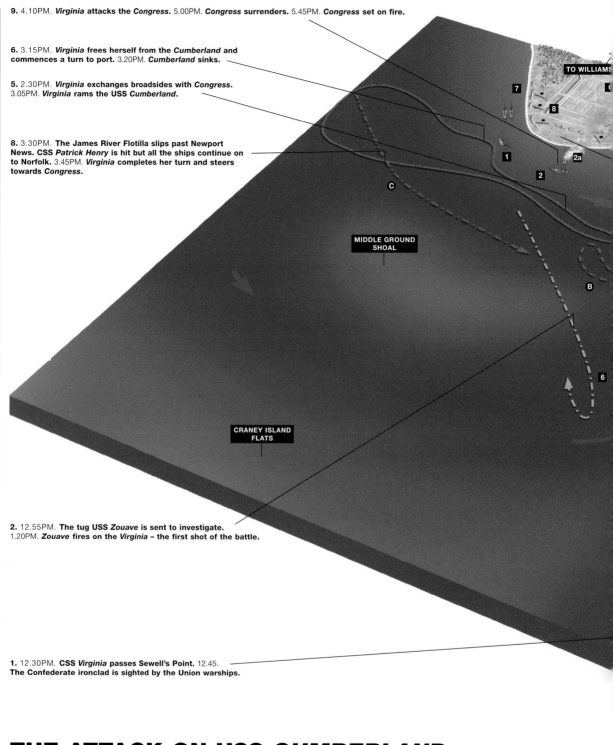

**9.** 4.10PM. *Virginia* attacks the *Congress*. 5.00PM. *Congress* surrenders. 5.45PM. *Congress* set on fire.

**6.** 3.15PM. *Virginia* frees herself from the *Cumberland* and commences a turn to port. 3.20PM. *Cumberland* sinks.

**5.** 2.30PM. *Virginia* exchanges broadsides with *Congress*. 3.05PM. *Virginia* rams the USS *Cumberland*.

**8.** 3.30PM. **The James River Flotilla slips past Newport News. CSS *Patrick Henry* is hit but all the ships continue on to Norfolk.** 3.45PM. *Virginia* completes her turn and steers towards *Congress*.

TO WILLIAMS

**7**

**8**

**1**

**2a**

**2**

C

MIDDLE GROUND SHOAL

B

**6**

CRANEY ISLAND FLATS

**2.** 12.55PM. **The tug USS *Zouave* is sent to investigate.** 1.20PM. *Zouave* fires on the *Virginia* – the first shot of the battle.

**1.** 12.30PM. **CSS *Virginia* passes Sewell's Point.** 12.45. **The Confederate ironclad is sighted by the Union warships.**

# THE ATTACK ON USS *CUMBERLAND* AND USS *CONGRESS*

8 March 1862, 12.30pm–5.45pm, viewed from the southeast, showing the CSS *Virginia*'s first attack on the Union blockading squadron, including the ramming of the USS *Cumberland* and the destruction of the USS *Congress*. The wind was 10mph from west-southwest throughout the action.

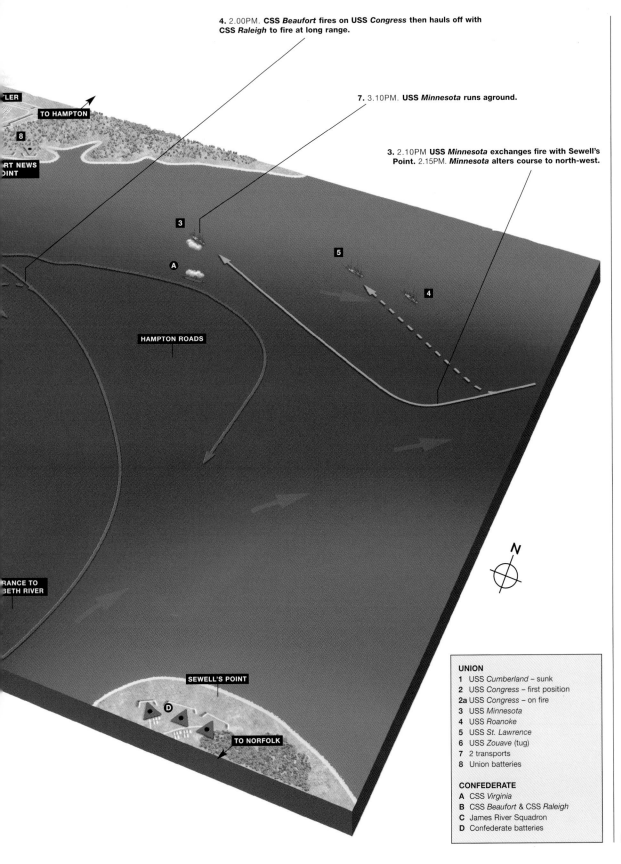

**4.** 2.00PM. **CSS** *Beaufort* fires on **USS** *Congress* then hauls off with **CSS** *Raleigh* to fire at long range.

**7.** 3.10PM. **USS** *Minnesota* runs aground.

**3.** 2.10PM **USS** *Minnesota* exchanges fire with Sewell's Point. 2.15PM. *Minnesota* alters course to north-west.

TO HAMPTON

'LER

8

RT NEWS
OINT

3

A

5

4

HAMPTON ROADS

RANCE TO
BETH RIVER

N

SEWELL'S POINT

D

TO NORFOLK

**UNION**
1   USS *Cumberland* – sunk
2   USS *Congress* – first position
2a  USS *Congress* – on fire
3   USS *Minnesota*
4   USS *Roanoke*
5   USS *St. Lawrence*
6   USS *Zouave* (tug)
7   2 transports
8   Union batteries

**CONFEDERATE**
A   CSS *Virginia*
B   CSS *Beaufort* & CSS *Raleigh*
C   James River Squadron
D   Confederate batteries

The ramming of the USS Cumberland by the CSS Virginia. While the two ships were locked together they continued to fire at each other at point-blank range. From "Battles and Leaders", 1894. (Hensley)

Captain Smith of the *Cumberland* recalled they bounced off the casemate "like India-rubber balls". By this stage the *Virginia* had closed to within 300 yards. She turned and presented her full starboard broadside to the frigate, then fired. The effect was devastating, particularly as her smoothbore guns had been loaded with heated shot. As Dr. Edward Shippen on the *Congress* recalled: "One of her shells dismounted an eight-inch gun and either killed or wounded every one of her gun's crew, while the slaughter at the other guns was fearful. There were comparatively few wounded, the fragments of the huge shells she threw killed outright as a general thing. Our clean and handsome gun-deck was in an instant changed into a slaughter-pen, with lopped-off legs and arms and bleeding, blackened bodies scattered about by the shells". She then fired a second broadside, overturning guns and sweeping men over the side. By this stage the two ships were so close that Frederick Curtis, the gun captain on one of the *Congress*'s 32-pdrs. thought that the *Virginia* was about to send over a boarding party. Paymaster Buchanan survived the broadside delivered at the orders of his brother. The crew of the *Congress* expected the *Virginia* to turn around and fire her port broadside, but she continued on her course, heading towards the *Cumberland*. The *Congress* was left burning from the heated shot, and her decks covered in blood and gore. Lieutenant Smith knew his ship was likely to sink under him, so he ordered her anchor cables to be cut and set his jib. He called on the tug *Zouave* to come to his aid, as he planned to beach his ship to prevent her from sinking. She ran aground in 17ft of water, effectively becoming a battered wooden fort, immobile but ready to fight. Pumps began to fight the fires, and the wounded were taken below for Dr. Shippen to tend. Her remaining crew watched the *Virginia* approach the *Cumberland*.

On the sloop the crew had rigged "springs", a system of anchors and cables that allowed the warship to be pulled around so she presented her broadside to the enemy. This also meant the *Virginia* was heading straight toward her beam amidships, in the ideal angle for a ramming attempt. The *Cumberland* opened fire with "a few forward 9-inch guns" and her 150-pdr. rifle. Both the heavy smoothbore shot and the 6in. rifled shot failed to penetrate the *Virginia*'s casemate, although they damaged her davits and rails. The *Virginia* opened fire on the *Cumberland* with her bow guns, while her starboard battery engaged the shore batteries on Newport News Point. The shore batteries replied, creating a hail of fire. On the *Gassendi*, Captain Gautier was "able to estimate the force of the fire, which during a quarter of an hour particularly, was of the hottest." This was the period around 3.00pm, when the *Virginia* was lining herself up to ram the *Cumberland*. Gautier continued, reporting that "we could see the entrance of the river constantly swept in all directions by the shot that ricocheted...." At first, the *Virginia* was able to rake the *Cumberland* as she approached, before the sloop was winched round on her "springs". Lieutenant Selfridge on the *Cumberland* described these raking shots as "a situation to shake the highest courage and the best discipline." He described the carnage:

Another depiction of the CSS *Virginia* ramming the USS *Cumberland*. Although the blow was a mortal wound for the Union warship, the ram jammed in the side of the Cumberland, and for a moment it appeared that the *Virginia* might be pulled under with her victim. (Author's Collection)

VIRGINIA SINKING THE CUMBERLAND, MARCH 8th 1862.

"The dead were thrown to the disengaged side of the deck; the wounded carried below. No one flinched, but everyone went on rapidly loading and firing; the places of the killed and wounded taken promptly by others…. The carnage was frightful. Great splinters torn from the ship's side and decks caused more casualties than the enemy's shell." By this time Buchanan had worked the *Virginia* into a position where she could ram her opponent. William Drake, the artillery volunteer, recalled hearing the order "Stand Fast! We are going to run into her!" As the *Virginia* surged forward, the engine room was given the signal to disengage her engines, then to go astern. Ramsay recalls: "There was an ominous pause, then a crash, shaking us all off our feet." To Lieutenant Jones, the *Virginia's* Executive Officer, "crashing timbers was distinctly heard above the din of battle." The 1,500lb iron ram bolted to the bow of the *Virginia* plowed into the side of the *Cumberland*, crushing her hull. The iron ram was buried deep inside the hull of the wooden sloop, which started to settle in the water. For a moment it seemed as if the *Cumberland* would take the *Virginia* down with her. The two ships were almost touching, and the *Cumberland* fired three broadsides in quick succession, the shot scraping down the ironclad's casemate. The shot shattered the muzzles of two of the *Virginia's* broadside smoothbores. Another shell hit the smokestack, causing "a terrible crash in the fire room," caused by the concussion. On the *Cumberland*, Lieutenant Selfridge described the view from the sloop. "Cheer after cheer went up from the *Cumberland*, only to be followed by exclamations of rage and despair as the enemy slowly moved away…." The *Virginia* had managed to free herself, leaving her ram embedded inside the *Cumberland*. Water rushed into the huge hole in her hull, which one witness described as being "wide enough to let in a horse and cart. The forward magazine was flooded … As the water gained the berth deck, which by this time was filled with the badly wounded, heart-rending cries above the din of combat could be heard from the poor fellows as they realized their helplessness to escape slow death from drowning." Both ships continued

The ramming of the USS *Cumberland* was a popular subject for maritime artists and contemporary engravers. A naval tactic from antiquity had been resurrected in an age of modern shell and armor. The *Virginia's* ram proved as deadly as her guns. (Mariners, courtesy of the Chrysler Museum of Art)

Commander John Randolph Tucker, CSN was the commander of the James River Squadron. Although his small flotilla ran past the batteries of Newport News Point on 8 March, his flagship, the CSS *Patrick Henry,* was damaged during the action (Museum of the Confederacy, Richmond, VA.)

to pour shot into each other, and as the *Virginia* backed away, the shore batteries added their weight to the barrage. A Confederate officer hailed the *Cumberland,* calling on her to surrender. Lieutenant Morris yelled the response: "Never! We will sink alongside with our colors flying." His ship was already doomed, as her decks were awash in blood and she was settling in the water. For some reason the *Virginia* rammed her again. The *Cumberland* was still firing, but she began to sway wildly as the *Virginia* pulled away again. A lucky shot from the sloop hit the bow gunport of the ironclad, killing two of the crew and wounding several more. These were the first Confederate casualties of the day. Morris gave the order to abandon ship, adding "Every man look out for himself!"

The crew began throwing themselves overboard, while a few of the wounded were lowered into boats. Lieutenant Selfridge was one of the last to abandon ship, but found his way to the upper deck blocked by an overweight drummer and his drum who was stuck in the hatch. He squirmed through a gunport instead, only to break the surface next to the musician, who was using his drum as a raft. As they struggled ashore, the survivors were offered whiskey and blankets. Observers on the *Congress* saw the confusion, and watched the *Cumberland* lurch, "then she went down like a bar of iron, but her flag still flew at her mast head; all was lost except honor." A Confederate observer declared her crew was "game to the last."

### "A terrible scene of carnage." The second attack on the *Congress*

It was now around 3.20pm. The *Virginia* had destroyed or damaged two powerful enemy warships, and was relatively unscathed. She was also facing in the opposite direction from the rest of the Union fleet. She continued bombarding the shore, destroying both the wharf and General Mansfield's headquarters. The *Virginia* had to turn to port, but it would take about 30 minutes to turn the ungainly ironclad through 180 degrees. In the meantime she provided enough of a distraction to allow the James River flotilla to steam past the Union batteries at Newport News. Following Buchanan's orders, Captain John R. Tucker's flagship, the CSS *Patrick Henry,* was "standing down James River under

Although inaccurate, as it combines both days of the battle into one scene, this lithograph gives a fair impression of the scene near Newport News Point on the first day, as the survivors from the *Cumberland* struggled ashore. In the foreground Brigadier General Mansfield is shown surveying the carnage. (Mariners)

full steam, accompanied by the *Jamestown* and *Teaser*. They were all nobly into action, and were soon exposed to heavy fire of the shore batteries." The *Patrick Henry* was hit several times, but managed to continue on with only minor damage, screening her consorts which were on her starboard side. The trio of gunboats continued on to the mouth of the Elizabeth River and the protection afforded by the batteries on Sewell's Point.

While the *Virginia* was busy attacking the two warships off Newport News, the other major warships in the blockading squadron tried to come to their aid. The *Minnesota* ran aground about 1½ miles east of Newport News Point. As the tide was ebbing, there was no chance of moving her for six hours. The *Roanoke* was duly towed back under the guns of Fort Monroe, while the *St. Lawrence* ran aground, but at least she was in a position where she could support the *Minnesota*. Buchanan recalled the problems he encountered turning his flagship. "I was obliged to run the ship a short distance above the batteries ... Thus we were subjected twice to the heavy guns of all the batteries in passing up and down the river, but it could not be avoided."

By 4.00pm she was back in position, her broadside facing the stern of the stranded *Congress*. The frigate was still on fire, and her decks were still filled with dead and wounded sailors. At a range of 150 yards the ironclad raked the frigate, overturning her remaining stern-firing guns and according to the ship's doctor, "Men were being killed and maimed every minute." He recalled how a line of cooks and stewards who were passing ammunition up from the hold were "raked by a shell, and the whole of them killed or wounded...." Captain Smith was amongst the casualties; killed by a splinter that sliced into his head. Lieutenant Austin Pendergast and Commander William Smith were now in command, and after almost 30 minutes of this carnage, the officers decided to surrender. Two white flags were raised and the *Virginia* ceased firing. It was just after 5.00pm. On the ironclad, Lieutenant Jones ordered his men to remain at their posts while Flag Officer Buchanan and several officers climbed onto the spar deck. Ramsey noted, "a pall of black smoke hung about the ships and obscured the clean-cut outlines of the shore. Down the river were the three frigates *St. Lawrence*,

A shell from the CSS *Virginia* penetrates the hull of the wooden sloop USS *Cumberland* and explodes inside her sick bay. Most of the wounded were unable to escape from below decks when the sloop sank. (Hensley)

*Roanoke* and *Minnesota.…* The masts of the *Cumberland* were protruding above the water. The *Congress* presented a terrible scene of carnage." A small boat was sent from the *Virginia* to the *Congress*, in itself a miracle given the damage to the deck fittings of the ironclad. Next, the *Beaufort* arrived to take the frigate's surviving officers off as prisoners, then burn the enemy ship. She was followed by the Confederate tug *Raleigh*. The two tugs had scarcely come alongside the *Congress* when they came under heavy fire from the shore. General Mansfield refused to support the frigate's peaceable surrender, and fired his batteries, supported by the rifle fire of two infantry companies. He ordered a subordinate to "send down marksmen and do not permit them to board the *Congress*." His actions were effectively a death warrant for the wounded sailors on board the frigate. Lieutenant Parker on the *Beaufort* recalled that bullets were hitting his tug "like hail." He withdrew to join two other Confederate tugs (*Harmony* and *Teaser*) that had just reached the scene,

Around 12.20am during the night of 8/9 March, the *Congress* finally exploded, after having burned all evening. It provided a dramatic finale to the events of the previous day, which demonstrated the vulnerability of wooden warships to modern shells. (VWM)

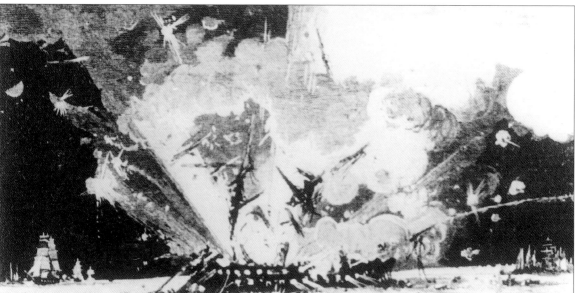

JACK: "Mr. Secretary! Mr. Secretary! Wake up! Here's the *Merrimac* got out and sunk the *Cumberland* and taken the *Congress!*"
MR. SECRETARY [Welles]: "Ah! (*yawns*) you don't say so? I must get Morgan to buy some more boats then!"

A contemporary cartoon in *Leslie's Weekly* ridicules the seeming lack of preparedness of Gideon Welles and the Navy Department to meet the threat posed by the CSS *Virginia*. The cartoon appeared before news of the clash between the ironclads had reached Washington. (Private Collection)

intent on capturing prisoners. The *Patrick Henry* made an attempt to divert the shore batteries, but her engines were hit by a shot from the *Minnesota*, releasing scalding steam into her engine room. The *Jamestown* towed her into Norfolk. By this time Flag Officer Buchanan had seen enough. He was still standing on the *Virginia*'s spar deck, watching the drama unfold. He ordered Jones to "plug hot shot into her and don't leave her until she's afire!" Just then he was hit in the groin by a rifle bullet. As he was carried below, he cried out: "That ship must be burned! They must look after their own wounded, since they won't let us!" Several heated shot were fired into the *Congress,* which was blazing from stem to stern. The crew abandoned ship while many of the wounded succumbed to the flames. Others escaped overboard, to be rescued by soldiers from the 20th Indiana. Paymaster Buchanan emerged unhurt but dazed, as did the surgeon, Dr. Shippen. An English observer described the burning *Congress* as a "helpless, hopeless charnel house."

Lieutenant Jones was now in command of the *Virginia,* and as the *Congress* was clearly burning, he turned his attention to the stranded *Minnesota,* 1½ miles away to the east. He quickly realized that the ironclad's draft was too deep to allow her to approach within close range of the Union frigate. He opened fire on the *Minnesota,* but it was getting harder to see the target as dusk approached. His pilots advised him to abandon the attack, as the water levels were dropping, and it was getting dark. Reluctantly Jones ordered his helmsman to steer toward the mouth of the Elizabeth River. It was 6.30pm, by 8.00pm the ironclad was riding at anchor, protected by the Confederate guns on Sewell's Point. Buchanan and the other wounded were taken ashore, along with the bodies of the two crewmen who had been killed. Union prisoners were

RIGHT **This somewhat stylized impression of the battle between the USS *Monitor* and the CSS *Virginia* on 9 March gives a good impression of the geography of Hampton Roads and the appearance of the ships that were there. At center left (18) is the French sloop *Gassendi*, lying between the main Union fleet and Sewell's Point. Newport News Point is shown in the upper right of the picture. (Smithsonian Institution, Washington D.C.)**

sent under guard to the Norfolk hospital, and Jones and his officers inspected their vessel for damage. The crew ate their evening meal around midnight, while Jones finished his report on the action. The Confederates had just inflicted a humiliating defeat on the US Navy, the worst day in its history since the capture of the USS *Chesapeake* in 1812. Over 2,650 sailors had been killed, and almost as many were wounded. The Navy had also lost two powerful warships, and the rest of their fleet lay exposed and vulnerable. Captain Gautier reported that; "Panic appeared to take possession of everyone. Several vessels changed their anchorage, and all held themselves in readiness to stand out to sea at the first movement of the enemy." Although the *St. Lawrence* was refloated, the *Minnesota* remained hard aground. She would be the obvious target when the *Virginia* resumed her attack in the morning.

The *Congress* had continued to burn all evening, and just after 12.30am she exploded "like a tremendous bombshell, and with a roar that could be heard for miles around." A Confederate witness described the end of the Union warship in "an enormous column of fire." A Union observer recalled that the sight "went straight to the marrow of our bones." Jones recounted that by the light of the flames, a Confederate pilot on the *Virginia* noticed "a strange-looking craft, brought out in bold relief by the light of the burning ship, which he at once proclaimed to be the Ericsson". His sighting was dismissed, and Jones continued to plan a second sortie to finish the piecemeal destruction of the entire blockading flotilla. In fact the pilot was correct. As the *Congress* burned, the *Monitor* steamed into Hampton Roads. After reporting to the squadron commander on board the *Roanoke*, Lieutenant Worden's ironclad was ordered to guard the *Minnesota*. When the battle was

**Captain Gersholm Jaques Van Brunt, USN, the Commanding Officer of the USS *Minnesota*, had the unenviable task of facing the CSS *Virginia* in an immobile wooden frigate. His vessel was saved by the actions of the USS *Monitor* on 9 March. (US Army Military History Institute)**

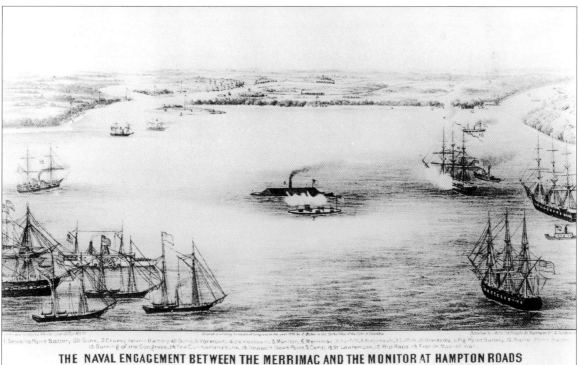

## THE NAVAL ENGAGEMENT BETWEEN THE MERRIMAC AND THE MONITOR AT HAMPTON ROADS
ON THE 9TH OF MARCH 1862.

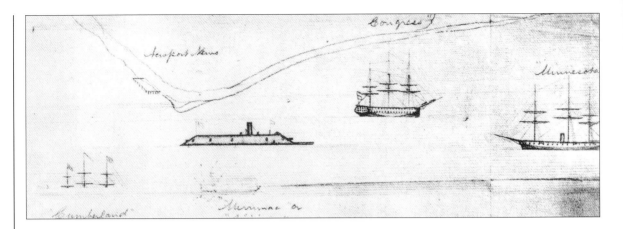

resumed the following morning, the Confederate ironclad would meet Ericsson's *Monitor*. Instead of fighting against unprotected wooden warships, the *Virginia* would be fighting another ironclad.

## "I WILL STAND BY YOU TO THE LAST"
### The first clash between the ironclads, Sunday 9 March 1862

In the predawn darkness, the *Virginia*'s officers examined their ship. Surgeon Philipps wrote: "I found all her stanchions, iron railings, boat davits and light work of every description swept away, her smokestack cut to pieces, two guns without muzzles, and 98 indentations on her plating, showing where heavy iron shot had struck, but glanced off without doing any injury." Water was also seeping in through a crack in the bow, caused when the iron ram had been wrenched off. Only Lieutenant Jones and the pilot knew of the possible presence of the *Monitor*, and everyone seemed to believe that the *Minnesota* would be the only real opponent that morning. The crew ate breakfast, which included "two jiggers of whiskey," then prepared for action. On the other side of Hampton Roads the *Monitor* had spent the night anchored alongside the *Minnesota*, "like some undersized sheepdog in the shadow of a very large but partially incapacitated ram." As the skies lightened, the crews of both vessels scanned the opposite sides of the Roads. Lieutenant Rochelle on the *Patrick Henry* observed that: "The *Minnesota* was discovered in her old position, but the *Minnesota* was not the only thing to attract attention. Close alongside of her lay such a craft as the eyes of a seaman never looked upon before – an immense shingle floating on the water, with a gigantic cheesebox rising from its center; no sails, no wheels, no smokestacks, no guns. What could it be"? Some thought it was a water raft, or a floating magazine. Others though she might be the *Monitor*. Lieutenant Jones seemed in little doubt. He told Lieutenant Hunter Davidson of "his determination to attack and ram her, and to keep vigorously at her until the contest was decided." On the *Monitor*, Lieutenant Worden spotted the "*Merrimack*" with several consorts at anchor off Sewell's Point. He also ordered his men to breakfast, then prepared his ship for action. Captain Jaques Van Brunt of the *Minnesota* was also getting his ship ready to face the *Virginia*. A cluster of tugs and small boats was busy removing her stores, baggage, even her paychest, in

A highly inaccurate view of the interior of the gundeck of the CSS *Virginia* appeared in the contemporary French publication *Le Monde Illustré*. The breech-loading gun, its carriage and even the uniforms are incorrect, but it retains something of the flavor of conditions inside a casemate battery. (Author's Collection)

The interior of the turret of the USS *Monitor*. Although somewhat inaccurate it was evidently based on experience, as the depiction of the gunport stoppers and their attendant pulley system is accurately shown. (VWM)

order to try to lighten the ship. There was a general assumption that she would be destroyed just like the *Cumberland* and *Congress*. Around 6.00am, Van Brunt saw the enemy "coming down from Craney Island." His men raced to their guns.

The *Virginia* had indeed slipped her mooring off Sewell's Point just before 6.00am, but a heavy bank of fog lay over Hampton Roads, and Lieutenant Jones wanted to wait until the tide had risen and the fog dispersed. He remained in station off the Point, while the sidewheel gunboats *Patrick Henry* and *Jamestown*, and the tug *Teaser* joined him. By 8.00am conditions had improved, and Jones conned his ship in the direction of Fort Wool preceded by the two gunboats before curving back toward the stranded *Minnesota*. The Union frigate lay two miles to the northwest, across the Roads. On the French sloop *Gassendi*, Captain Gautier reported that: "at eight-o-clock the fog completely disappeared." Van Brunt and Lieutenant Worden saw the move, and exchanged a last

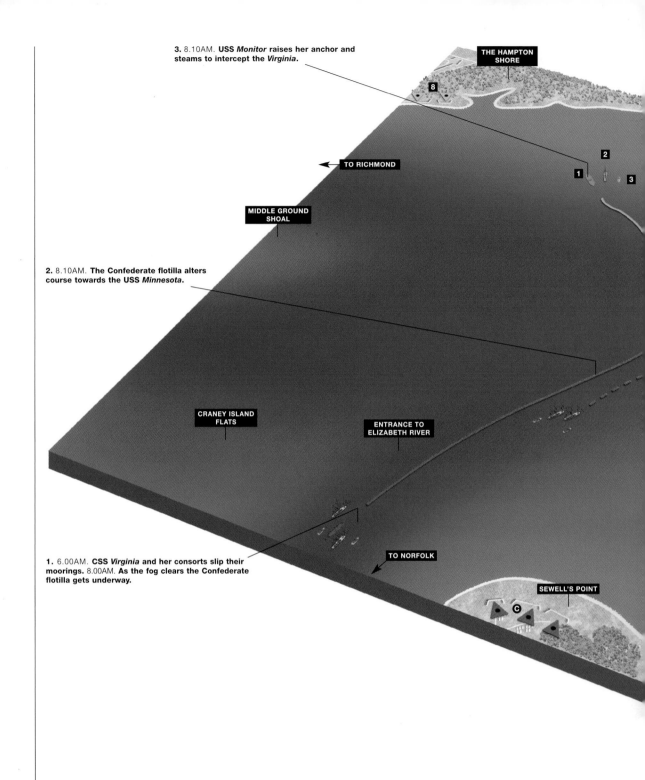

**3.** 8.10AM. **USS** *Monitor* **raises her anchor and steams to intercept the** *Virginia*.

THE HAMPTON SHORE

TO RICHMOND

MIDDLE GROUND SHOAL

**2.** 8.10AM. **The Confederate flotilla alters course towards the USS** *Minnesota*.

CRANEY ISLAND FLATS

ENTRANCE TO ELIZABETH RIVER

**1.** 6.00AM. **CSS** *Virginia* **and her consorts slip their moorings.** 8.00AM. **As the fog clears the Confederate flotilla gets underway.**

TO NORFOLK

SEWELL'S POINT

# THE BATTLE OF HAMPTON ROADS

9 March 1862, 6.00am–10.00am, viewed from the southeast. CSS *Virginia* returns to finish off the Union blockading squadron, in particular the USS *Minnesota*. The *Virginia* is intercepted by the Union ironclad USS *Monitor*, however, and their epic confrontation begins. Wind is 5mph from the west throughout the morning.

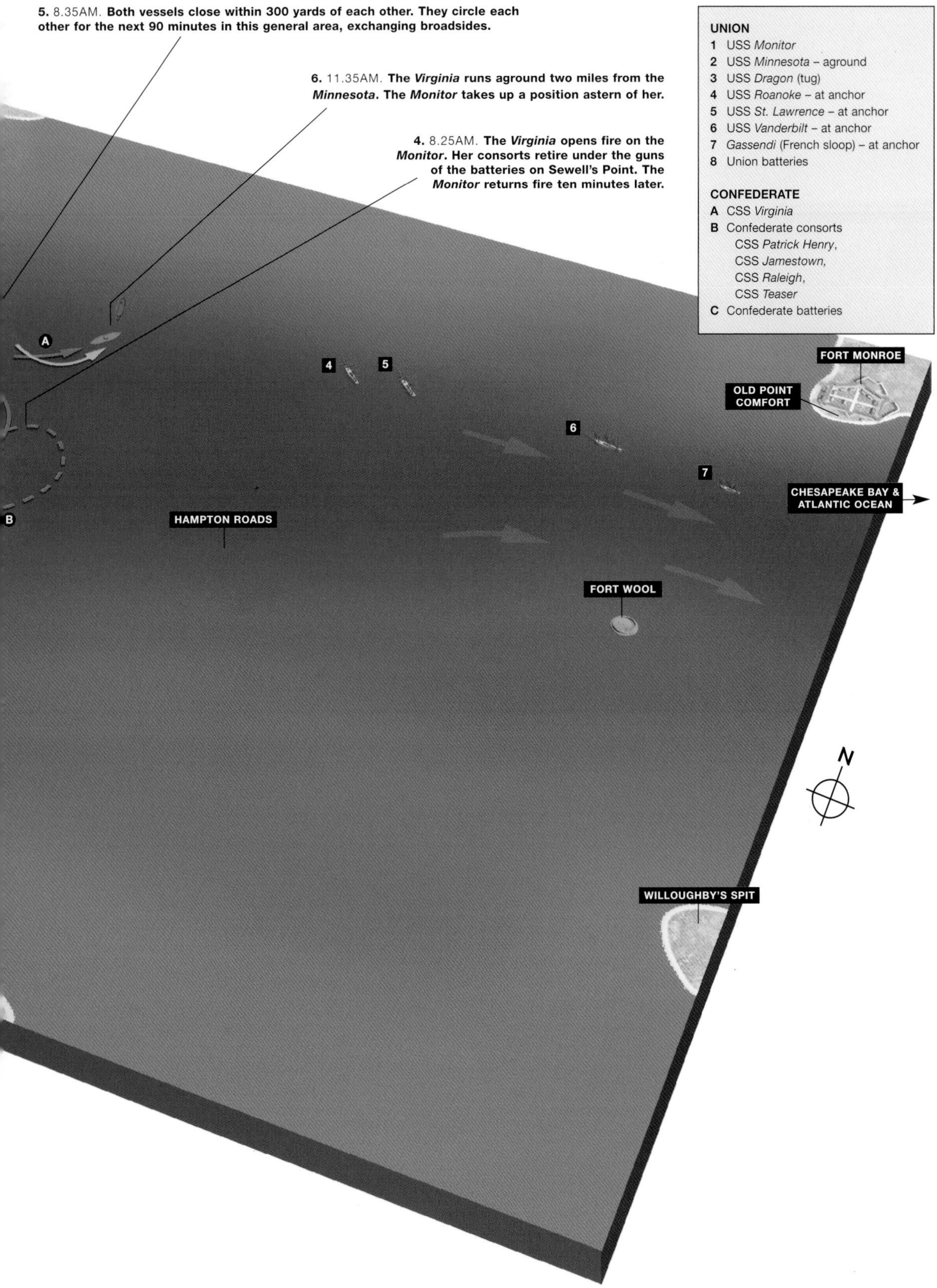

**5.** 8.35AM. **Both vessels close within 300 yards of each other. They circle each other for the next 90 minutes in this general area, exchanging broadsides.**

**6.** 11.35AM. **The *Virginia* runs aground two miles from the *Minnesota*. The *Monitor* takes up a position astern of her.**

**4.** 8.25AM. **The *Virginia* opens fire on the *Monitor*. Her consorts retire under the guns of the batteries on Sewell's Point. The *Monitor* returns fire ten minutes later.**

**UNION**
1 USS *Monitor*
2 USS *Minnesota* – aground
3 USS *Dragon* (tug)
4 USS *Roanoke* – at anchor
5 USS *St. Lawrence* – at anchor
6 USS *Vanderbilt* – at anchor
7 *Gassendi* (French sloop) – at anchor
8 Union batteries

**CONFEDERATE**
A CSS *Virginia*
B Confederate consorts
   CSS *Patrick Henry*,
   CSS *Jamestown*,
   CSS *Raleigh*,
   CSS *Teaser*
C Confederate batteries

A

B

4

5

6

7

**FORT MONROE**

**OLD POINT COMFORT**

**CHESAPEAKE BAY & ATLANTIC OCEAN** →

**HAMPTON ROADS**

**FORT WOOL**

N

**WILLOUGHBY'S SPIT**

This atmospheric engraving is probably the most accurate depiction of conditions inside the turret of the USS *Monitor* that was produced by contemporary artists. Eighteen men and two 15,700lb guns and their slide carriages were crammed into the 20ft diameter space. The conditions during action could only be described as "hellish". (VWM)

OPPOSITE TOP

In this contemporary depiction of the scene inside the USS *Monitor*'s turret, the gun crew is shown peering out through the gun port, waiting for the CSS *Virginia* to appear in their line of sight. (Hensley)

OPPOSITE BOTTOM

Although inaccurate, this detailed engraving shows the final moments of the battle, just before a shot from the stern gun of the CSS *Virginia* hit the USS *Monitor*'s pilot house. Although several other ships are included in the scene, the closest wooden vessel to the action was the USS *Minnesota*, stranded over a mile to the north. (VWM)

few words before they went into action. The captain of the *Minnesota* told Worden: "If I cannot lighten my ship off, I will destroy her." Worden replied: "I will stand by you to the last if I can help you." Van Brunt's thoughts on the *Monitor* probably mirrored those of Dr. Shippen, watching from Fort Monroe: "she seemed so small and trifling that we feared she would only constitute additional prey for the leviathan."

When the *Virginia* was a mile away from the *Minnesota*, the Union vessel opened fire with her stern guns. Others claim that the *Virginia* fired first, while Captain Tucker commanding the *Virginia*'s consorts recorded that his gunboats opened the engagement. William Keeler, the paymaster of the *Monitor*, was watching from the ironclad's deck, and wrote that the *Virginia* fired, and "a shell howled over our heads and crashed into the side of the *Minnesota*." Worden ordered everyone to go below. It was shortly before 8.30am. After the *Virginia* fired, Worden reported that: "I got underway as soon as possible and stood directly for her, with the crew at quarters, in order to meet and engage her as far away from the *Minnesota* as possible." Van Brunt wrote that the *Monitor* "laid herself right alongside of the *Merrimack*, and the contrast was that of a pigmy to a giant." As Ashton Ramsay, the *Virginia*'s Chief Engineer recalled, "suddenly to our astonishment a black object that looked like… a barrelhead afloat with a cheesebox on top of it moved slowly out from under the *Minnesota* and boldly confronted us."

In the *Monitor*'s turret, Lieutenant Greene supervised the loading of the twin 11in. Dahlgrens with solid shot. Each gun was crewed by eight men, while Greene and Acting Master Louis N. Stodder supervised their operation. These two men had some idea of what was going on, as they could see out of the gunports. The only other viewpoint on the *Monitor* was the pilot house, where the Pilot, Samuel Howard, and the Quartermaster, Peter Williams, accompanied Lieutenant Worden. Williams manned the ship's wheel. As the speaking tube linking turret to pilot house had broken down, Worden in the pilot house and Greene in the turret could only communicate by message carriers in the berth deck. Paymaster Keeler volunteered to maintain the link between the two parts of the ship. He was assisted by Captain's Clerk Daniel Toffey. Greene called down: "Paymaster, ask the captain if I shall fire!"

The reply came back: "Tell Mr. Greene not to fire till I give the word, to be cool and deliberate, to take sure aim and not waste a shot". The gunboats peeled away from the *Virginia* as the two ironclads approached each other, returning to lie underneath the guns on Sewell's Point. As the Frenchman Gautier put it: "they were seen to abandon the attack and retire under the batteries of Sewell's, leaving the *Merrimack* to defend alone the honor of their young flag." When the two were within

This representation of the battle between the two ironclads on 9 March contains a number of errors, but it accurately shows the superficial damage inflicted on the deck fittings of the CSS *Virginia*. Her smokestack, deck rails and boat davits had been severely damaged during the previous day's engagement. (Hensley)

100 yards of each other, Worden turned the *Monitor* so her bows faced upstream, taking the way off the ship. He then gave the order to open fire. Greene decided to fire the first shot himself. "I triced up the port, ran out the gun, and taking deliberate aim, pulled the lockstring." The *Monitor* shuddered under the impact. Observers thought the first shot hit the *Virginia* "plumb on the waterline." Jones was in the process of turning his ship to starboard, which presented his full broadside to the enemy. Both ships were now parallel to each other, but headed in opposite directions; the *Monitor* facing west and the *Virginia* east. He gave the order to fire. According to Greene, it was "a rattling broadside … the turret and other parts of the ship were heavily struck, but the shots did not penetrate; the tower was intact, and it continued to revolve."

Greene later wrote that "a look of confidence passed over the men's faces, and we believed the *Merrimack* would not repeat the work she had accomplished the day before." One gunner even thought the Confederates were firing canister at them, as the shots "rattled on our iron decks like hailstones."

Worden recalled that "at this period I felt some anxiety about the turret machinery, it having been predicted by many persons that a heavy shot with great initial velocity striking the turret would so derange it as to stop its working; but finding that it had been twice struck and still revolved as freely as ever, I turned back with renewed confidence and hope, and continued the engagement at close quarters; every shot from our guns taking effect on the high sides of our adversary, stripping off the iron freely." This was the ultimate test of Ericsson's invention. Both the *Monitor*'s hull and turret armor were proof to the rifled shot fired by her opponent.

Worden "passed slowly by her, within a few yards, delivering fire as rapidly as possible and receiving from her a rapid fire in return, both from her great guns and musketry – the latter aimed at the pilot house, hoping undoubtedly to penetrate through the lookout holes and to disable the commanding officer and the helmsman."

Although the *Virginia* maintained a heavy fire, its shot seemed to be incapable of damaging the *Monitor*. Officers in the attendant flotilla of Confederate vessels near Sewell's Point were heard to say "the unknown craft was a wicked thing, and that we better not get too near her." It was becoming increasingly apparent that the *Virginia* had met her match. This ineffectiveness frustrated Jones, who recalled, "she and her turret appeared to be in perfect control. Her light draft enabled her to move about us at pleasure. She once took position for a short while where we could not bring a gun to bear on her." Jones would have been relieved to know that the heavy smoothbore guns on the *Monitor* were firing using reduced charges, a safety precaution that reduced velocity at short range. The *Monitor* was firing 168lb solid roundshot using 15lb of gunpowder to propel the shot, two thirds of the normal charge. This reduction in powder was made in accordance with the instructions of Captain John A. Dahlgren, the inventor of the *Monitor*'s guns, and the Chief of Naval Ordnance. He was concerned that the guns could burst if fired using a larger charge, but subsequent tests proved the reliability of his guns.

If the *Monitor* had used full charges of gunpowder, her shots might have had more chance of penetrating the *Virginia*'s lighter armor. Ramsay recalled that; "we hovered about each other in spirals, gradually contracting the circuits until we were within point-blank range, but our shell glanced from the *Monitor*'s turret just as hers did from our sloping sides". These sloping sides were angled inward at 35 degrees from the vertical. The *Virginia*'s designer, John L. Porter, and ordnance expert, John M. Brooke, worked out that this was the optimal angle of deflection to confound incoming roundshot, while retaining enough space inside the casemate to house the battery. The same angle was used in almost all subsequent Confederate casemate ironclads, as the theory was proved in battle. The 11in. roundshot fired by the *Monitor*'s two guns tended to strike the casemate, and were then deflected upwards by the slope. This significantly reduced the effect of the impact, and rendered the *Virginia* relatively impervious to enemy fire. The weakness with the casemate design was also becoming apparent. Two layers of two-inch-thick metal plate protected her casemate. These were bolted into place on top of a wooden frame, and although the armor was thick enough to

**Another stylized 20th-century depiction of the Battle of Hampton Roads, this painting manages to include the sinking of the CSS *Cumberland* into an otherwise correct representation of the second day's battle. (Casemate)**

ABOVE, RIGHT **Photographed some months after the battle, the turret of the USS Monitor still bears the scars of battle. Note the improved pilot house in the background, built to replace the simple box structure destroyed during the battle. The officers posing for the photo are Lieutenants A.B. Campbell** (left) **and L.P. Flyle, USN** (right). **(US Navy)**

withstand the enemy shot, each hit caused damage to the retaining bolts. Both Worden and Greene noticed this, and thought it possible that by concentrating their fire at a particular spot, sections of the armor plating could be shot away. Another problem with the *Virginia* was her armament. Two of her 9in. smoothbores had been damaged in the previous day's battle, and although they could still be fired even though their muzzles had been shot away, they were wildly inaccurate. The minor damage to her forward-facing 7in. Brooke rifle had been repaired by the time the battle began, and the piece appeared to function normally during the engagement with the *Monitor*.

More serious was her shortage of appropriate ammunition. The previous day, when she sailed out to fight the wooden ships of the blockading squadron, her solid cast-iron roundshot had been left behind, as it was less effective against unarmored opponents. Her ammunition had not been replenished, and when she steamed into battle against the *Monitor* she only had explosive shells in her magazines, apart from canister, which was an anti-personnel projectile. She also had the facilities to fire heated shot, which proved useful the day before, but was of no value in her fight against another ironclad. As her Chief Engineer related: "If we had known we were to meet her, we would have been supplied with solid shot for our rifled cannons." Another officer wrote: "our only hope to penetrate the *Monitor*'s shield was in the rifled cannon, but as the only projectiles we had for those were percussion shells, there was barely a chance that we might penetrate our adversary's defense by a lucky shot." Jones was well aware of the problem, and although he had every faith in the superb rifled guns that had been designed by John M. Brooke, he knew that only a very lucky shot would have any effect on his opponent. Later in the day a shot from one of his Brooke rifles would prove his faith was well placed. If his guns were relatively ineffective against the *Monitor*, Jones still retained the perfect means of destroying the wooden frigate *Minnesota*, so this remained his priority throughout the morning. Similarly, Worden's objective was to keep the *Virginia* as far away from the frigate as possible. To the observers lining both shores of Hampton Roads, the duel between the two ironclads appeared ferocious. William E. Rogers of the 10th New York Regiment felt that "truly this odd little craft was no match for this great monster. They closed in, however, and a curtain of smoke settled down over the scene with the Confederate batteries on Sewell's Point, Pig Point and Craney Island in the fray. With breathless suspense we listened to this firing, but could see nothing for the clouds of smoke. We heard the whistle of the shells and the shot, and we could recognize the shots of the *Monitor*. One takes no note of time under such circumstances. How long that first round lasted before the firing ceased I have no idea. When the thunder ceased, oh! We thought the 'cheesebox' had gone to the bottom. Gradually the smoke lifted and there lay the two antagonists, backing, filling and jockeying for position, then at it again, and again the cloud of smoke which settled over their struggle hid them from view."

Lieutenant John Taylor Wood, CSN fired the last shot of the battle. The conical shell fired from the CSS *Virginia*'s stern 7in. Brooke's Rifle hit the USS *Monitor*'s pilot house and wounded Lieutenant Worden. (VWM)

The conflict was also a confusing one for those taking part. In the *Virginia*, Ramsay recalled that "on our gun deck all was bustle, smoke, grimy figures and stern commands, while down in the engine and boiler rooms the sixteen furnaces were belching out fire and smoke, and the firemen standing in front of them like so many gladiators, tugging away with devil's claw and slice-bar, inducing by their exertions more and more intense combustion and heat. The noise of the crackling, roaring fires, escaping steam, and the loud and labored pulsations of the engines, together with the roar of battle above, and the thud and vibration of the huge masses of iron which were hurled against us produced a scene and sound to be compared only with the poet's picture of the lower regions."

Conditions were as bad, if not worse, on board the *Monitor*, and at one stage Lieutenant Worden had to clamber out onto the open deck to look around, assess the damage inflicted on his ship, and to get his bearings. This display of calm bravery under fire was typical of the man who Acting Master John Webber described as being "as cool as a man playing a game of chess." While he was standing there he was subjected to volleys of musket fire from the *Virginia*, the bullets flying "as thick as hailstones in a storm". He noted the turret bore the dents from the conical shells fired by the *Virginia*'s Brooke rifles. The 68lb projectiles created 4in. dents in the sides of the turret, but failed to cause any real damage. Even these non-penetrating shots could be dangerous, although the armor was sufficient to protect the turret crew. Acting Master Stodder was busy operating the machinery that rotated the turret. As he leaned against the turret side the structure was hit by one of these non-penetrating rounds. He was stunned by the vibration, and had to be carried below, suffering from concussion. He was replaced by Chief Engineer Alban C. Stimers, the man who had supervised the ironclad's construction on behalf of the Navy Department. Although her armored protection proved more than adequate, other features of Ericsson's design proved less reliable. The lack of communication between turret and pilot house was a significant problem, and however quickly messages could be relayed from one position to the other, it was still too slow to be able to react to events with any degree of alacrity. Another problem was that both the Paymaster and the Captain's Clerk

were not real sailors or gunners, so lacked the technical vocabulary to perform their job properly. As Lieutenant Greene later described it: "The situation was novel: a vessel of war was engaged in desperate combat with a powerful foe, the captain, commanding and guiding, was enclosed in one place, and the Executive Officer, working and fighting the guns, was shut up in another."

Lieutenant Greene described the situation inside the *Monitor*'s turret. "My only view of the world outside the tower was over the muzzles of the guns, which cleared the ports by only a few inches. When the guns were run in, the portholes were covered by heavy iron pendulums, pierced with small holes to allow the iron rammer and sponge handles to protrude while they were in use. To hoist these pendulums required the entire gun's crew and vastly increased the work inside the turret." Eighteen men were trapped inside a smoke-filled metal box 20ft in diameter, and filled with two massive guns. They were also under near-constant fire, as marksmen tried to fire in through the gun ports, and the *Virginia*'s shells tried to penetrate the turret, the rounds clanging into its sides and shaking the whole structure. Green recalled that: "the effect upon one shut up in a revolving drum is perplexing, and it is not a simple matter to keep the bearings. White marks had been placed upon the stationary deck immediately below the turret to indicate the direction of the starboard and port sides, and the bow and the stern; but these marks were obliterated early in the action. I would continually ask the captain, 'How does the *Merrimac* bear?' He replied 'On the starboard beam', or 'on the port quarter", as the case might be. Then, the difficulty was to determine the direction of the starboard beam or port quarter, or any other bearing."

The gun crews had no idea where the enemy was most of the time, let alone which direction their own ship was pointing. After a few rounds, Greene developed a solution that solved both the problem of the cumbersome gun port covers and the confusion over direction. "It finally resulted, that when a gun was ready for firing, the turret would be

Another photograph of the crew of the USS *Monitor* relaxing on deck while at anchor in the James River. The photograph was taken on 9 July, exactly four months after her clash with the CSS *Virginia*. (US Navy)

started on its revolving journey in search of the target, and when found it was taken 'on the fly', because the turret could not be accurately controlled." In other words, Greene's solution was to keep the gun port covers open all the time. When a gun had fired, he ordered the turret to be turned, so the open ports faced away from the enemy. Protected by the bulk of the turret itself, the gun was then reloaded and run out again. Greene would then give the order to turn the turret, and he peered through the small gap around the muzzle until the *Virginia* filled his view. He then pulled the lanyard and fired the gun. During the action he elected to fire each gun himself, moving constantly from gun to gun throughout the action.

Below the *Monitor*'s turret, Paymaster Keeler was unable to see the action develop, but he heard everything, and both Worden and Greene kept him abreast of developments as they relayed information from one part of the ship to the other. Keeler wrote: "The sounds of the conflict were terrible. The rapid fire of our guns amid the clouds of smoke, the howling of the *Minnesota's* shells, which were firing broadsides just over our heads (two of her shots struck us), mingled with the terrible crash of solid shot against our sides (not from the *Virginia*) and the bursting of shells all around us. Two men had been sent down from the turret, knocked senseless by balls striking outside the turret while they happened to be in contact with the inside wall of the turret". In a letter to his wife Anna, he recalled some of the orders passed back and forth. "Tell Mr. Greene that I am going to bring him on our Starboard beam, close alongside," or, "They're going to board us, put in a round of canister." He also passed on Worden's comments about the shooting; "That was a good shot, went through her waterline," or, "That last shot brought iron from her sides".

### "A moment of terrible suspense." The battle of maneuver

After two hours of dueling, both captains were beginning to realize that they had little chance of damaging their opponent through gunfire alone. While Jones had the option of trying to maneuver closer to the *Minnesota* to attack her, both captains could also try to ram their opponent. The duel

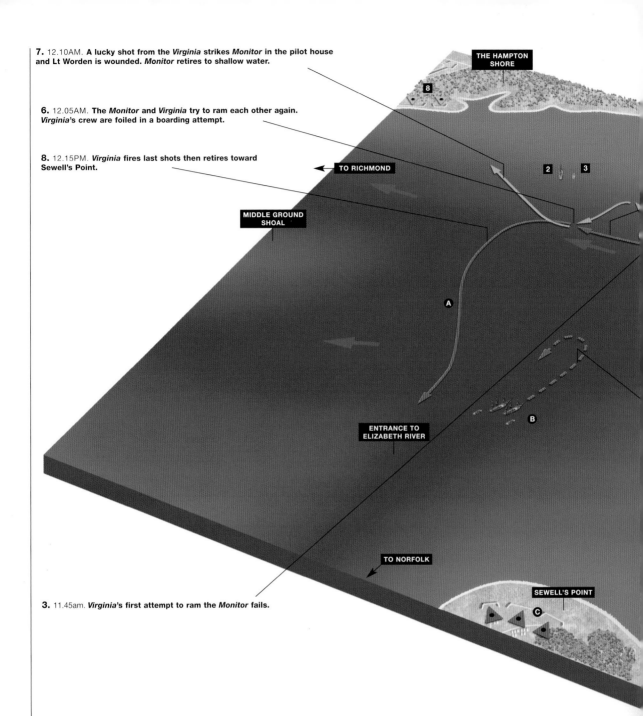

**7.** 12.10AM. **A lucky shot from the** *Virginia* **strikes** *Monitor* **in the pilot house and Lt Worden is wounded.** *Monitor* **retires to shallow water.**

THE HAMPTON SHORE

**6.** 12.05AM. **The** *Monitor* **and** *Virginia* **try to ram each other again.** *Virginia*'s **crew are foiled in a boarding attempt.**

**8.** 12.15PM. *Virginia* **fires last shots then retires toward Sewell's Point.**

← TO RICHMOND

MIDDLE GROUND SHOAL

ENTRANCE TO ELIZABETH RIVER

TO NORFOLK

SEWELL'S POINT

**3.** 11.45am. *Virginia*'s **first attempt to ram the** *Monitor* **fails.**

# THE BATTLE OF HAMPTON ROADS

9 March 1862, 11.40am–12.15pm, viewed from the southeast. With *Virginia* having freed herself, the two vessels make various attempts to ram and board each other. A lucky shot strikes the pilot house of the USS *Monitor*, wounding Lt Worden. The *Monitor* retires to shallow water and, with the water levels falling, *Virginia* retires towards Sewell's Point. Wind is 5mph from west-northwest; it shifted at around 10.15am.

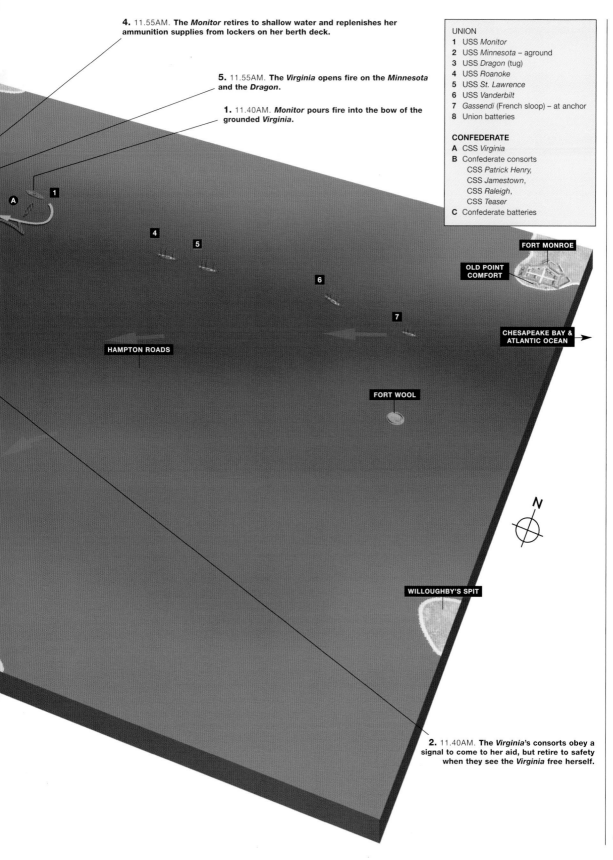

**4.** 11.55AM. **The *Monitor* retires to shallow water and replenishes her ammunition supplies from lockers on her berth deck.**

**5.** 11.55AM. **The *Virginia* opens fire on the *Minnesota* and the *Dragon*.**

**1.** 11.40AM. ***Monitor* pours fire into the bow of the grounded *Virginia*.**

UNION
1  USS *Monitor*
2  USS *Minnesota* – aground
3  USS *Dragon* (tug)
4  USS *Roanoke*
5  USS *St. Lawrence*
6  USS *Vanderbilt*
7  *Gassendi* (French sloop) – at anchor
8  Union batteries

CONFEDERATE
A  CSS *Virginia*
B  Confederate consorts
      CSS *Patrick Henry*,
      CSS *Jamestown*,
      CSS *Raleigh*,
      CSS *Teaser*
C  Confederate batteries

**A**

**1**

**4**

**5**

**6**

**7**

FORT MONROE

OLD POINT COMFORT

CHESAPEAKE BAY & ATLANTIC OCEAN

HAMPTON ROADS

FORT WOOL

N

WILLOUGHBY'S SPIT

**2.** 11.40AM. **The *Virginia*'s consorts obey a signal to come to her aid, but retire to safety when they see the *Virginia* free herself.**

**79**

The Union blockading fleet, including the USS *Monitor*, is shown retiring behind the guns of Fort Monroe during the sortie of the CSS *Virginia* on 8 May 1862 in this early 20th-century rendition. (US Navy)

continued, but instead of a contest between two ships steaming in circles around each other, around 11.00am Jones and Worden began to try other stratagems. Of the two ships, the *Monitor* was by far the more maneuverable, and Worden decided to try to ram the stern of her opponent, hoping to damage her screw (propeller) or rudder. If the *Virginia* could be disabled, then the *Monitor* could find a blind spot and pour fire into her without danger. First, Worden had to deal with a logistical problem. His guns had run out of ammunition, and in order to replenish the supplies within the turret, he had to disengage, and steam away from his opponent. Shot was brought up out of the hold, and while this was going on, Jones edged his ship closer to the *Minnesota*. Both he and his pilot were unsure of how deep the water was beneath their keel, and by the time they had charted a course to get as close to the wooden frigate as they could, the *Monitor* was steaming back into the fray. Worden made a dash for the *Virginia*'s stern, but missed by just two feet. Jones also decided to break the circling pattern adopted by the two ships in an attempt to attack the *Minnesota*. He steered northwest, forcing the *Monitor* to chase after him, and try to cut in between the *Virginia* and the stranded frigate. Just at that moment, in Lieutenant Jones's words, "In spite of all the cares of our pilots, we ran ashore". The surgeon, Dr. Phillips, was less reluctant to place blame: "the pilot purposely ran us aground nearly two miles off from the *Minnesota*, fearing that frigate's terrible broadside." This was a potential disaster for the Confederates, and Worden was quick to take advantage of their plight. He laid his ship alongside the *Virginia* so that the smaller ironclad lay beneath the muzzles of the Confederate

Union troops under the command of General Wool shown embarking at Fort Monroe for the amphibious assault on Norfolk. A beachhead was established on Willoughby's Spit, visible in the left background. (Casemate)

OVERLEAF
**THE CSS *VIRGINIA* ATTEMPTS TO RAM THE USS *MONITOR*, 9 MARCH 1862**
After the first hour or so of duelling between the two ironclads, both commanders were running out of options. It had become clear that the under-charged propellant used on the USS *Monitor* was insufficient to allow its 11in. roundshot to penetrate the *Virginia*'s armor. Similarly, the hollow shells used on the CSS *Virginia* were unable to do more than dent the turret of her opponent. Lieutenant Catesby ap Jones had just pulled his ship off a mudbank, and found that the *Monitor* was lying off his bow. He ordered for full steam in an attempt to ram his adversary, but without his iron ram, he was reluctant to damage his own ship. Consequently he reversed his engines immediately before the collision, and the glancing blow to the *Monitor* did little damage. Although accounts vary (one claims the blow struck the *Monitor*'s starboard beam), the scene depicts the *Virginia* striking a glancing blow to the *Monitor*'s stern, on her port quarter. (Adam Hook)

guns. As Van Brunt described it; "the contrast was that of a pygmy to a giant." Phillips recalled that "she directed a succession of shots at the same section of our vessel, and some of them striking close together, started the timbers and drove them perceptibly in … she began to sound every chink in our armor – every one but that which was actually vulnerable, had she known it." He was referring to the waterline. As the *Virginia* burned coal, she became lighter, and consequently her protective knuckle at the bottom of the casemate rose closer to the surface. It was designed to extend almost three feet below the waterline. After two days of fighting, it was only six inches below the surface. As Ramsay reported: "Lightened as we were, these exposed portions rendered us no longer an ironclad, and the *Monitor* might have pierced us between wind and water had she depressed her gun." Worden was oblivious to the opportunity this presented.

With the *Virginia* aground, Jones tried everything he could to move her off the mud bank. Ramsay was the man of the moment. "We lashed down the safety valves, heaped quick-burning combustibles into the already raging fires, and brought the boilers to a pressure that would be unsafe under ordinary circumstances. The propeller churned the mud and water furiously, but the ship did not stir. We piled on oiled cotton waste, splits of wood, anything that would burn faster than coal. It seemed impossible that the boilers could stand the pressure we were crowding upon them. Just as we were beginning to despair, there was a perceptible movement, and the *Merrimack* slowly dragged herself off the shoal by main strength. We were saved." To the crew, this seemed a miracle. By placing everyone at risk by straining the engines and boilers almost beyond endurance, Ramsay managed to develop enough reverse thrust to drag the vessel back into open water.

Minutes before, Jones had ordered his yeoman to signal the wooden consorts lying off Sewell's Point. When Captain Tucker saw the signal "my screw is disabled", he realized that by going to the rescue of the ironclad, he would be sacrificing his ship. As his Executive Officer, Lieutenant Rochelle, put it, "No wooden vessel could have floated twenty minutes under the fire the *Virginia* was undergoing, but if her propeller was disabled it was necessary to tow her back to the cover of our batteries, so the *Patrick Henry* and *Jamestown* started to make the attempt." The crews of the two gunboats must have been immensely

Major General Benjamin Huger, the commander of the Department of Norfolk, abandoned the city and destroyed the Navy Yard without informing Flag Officer Tattnal, who commanded the CSS *Virginia* at the time. His actions led directly to the loss of the ironclad. (Museum of the Confederacy, Richmond, VA.)

relieved to see the ironclad pull herself off without help. While all this was going on, Lieutenant Jones passed through the ship, visiting every gun crew. He noticed that the division of two smoothbore guns commanded by Lieutenant J.R. Eggleston had ceased firing. When asked why his guns were not returning the fire of the *Monitor*, Eggleston replied with the perfect summation of the gunnery duel: "Why, our powder is very precious, and after two hours incessant firing I find that I can do her about as much damage by snapping my thumb every two minutes and a half." Jones decided not to press the matter. What Eggleston had said was perfectly true.

If it was too difficult to approach the *Minnesota* without running aground, and if his gunnery was ineffective, Jones had one other tactical option. He could ram the *Monitor*. Using the ship herself as a weapon had worked well the day before, but the *Cumberland* was a stationary target, and as one critic on board put it, the *Virginia* "was as unwieldy as Noah's Ark." It took the better part of an hour to maneuver into a position where the *Virginia* could ram her opponent. After a run of half a mile, Jones was on target. Worden called out to Keeler: "Look out now, they're going to run us down! Give them both guns!" He also turned the ship, which almost escaped the collision completely. What followed was described by the Paymaster as "a moment of terrible suspense." The *Virginia* caught the *Monitor* a glancing blow, "nearly throwing us from our feet," as Keeler recalled. Jones had reversed the engines immediately before impact, which reduced the effect of the collision on both ships. The *Monitor* "spun around like a top." All he managed to do was to dent the hull of the *Monitor*, but the blow produced a leak in the bow of the Confederate vessel. As the *Virginia* plowed past the *Monitor*, Greene fired both his guns, driving in the armor protecting the stern of the casemate. A second hit in the same spot would probably have penetrated the hull. Jones was more concerned with the leak, and rigged pumps to deal with the flooding. He was also running out of options. For a moment he considered boarding. A group of volunteers was organized, led by Captain Reuben T. Thom, commander of the *Virginia*'s marines. Thom planned to jump onto the *Monitor* when the opportunity presented itself.

Unable to escape up the James River to the safety of Richmond because of her deep draft, the *Virginia* was burned and scuttled by her own crew off Craney Island early on the morning of 11 May 1862. (Hensley)

Robert E. Lee's son Colonel Custis W. Lee fortified Drewry's Bluff, overlooking the James River. When Norfolk fell, the fortification was all that lay between the Union fleet and Richmond. The gun shown in the photograph is a 10in. Columbiad smoothbore. (US Army Military History Institute)

Once on board his men would throw a coat over the slits in the pilot house, and jam the turret using metal spikes. Worden obviously took the threat seriously, as at one stage he ordered Greene to load his guns with canister. He had seen the boarding party gathering on the *Virginia's* spar deck. The *Monitor* dropped astern, and the opportunity passed. Thom ordered his men back to their guns. About this time the Confederate ensign was shot away, raising a cheer from the Union soldiers watching the fight from the shore. A replacement ensign was rigged and the fight continued, with Jones edging as close as he dared to the *Minnesota*. One shot struck the boiler of the tug USS *Dragon*, which was lying alongside the frigate. Other shots burst inside the *Minnesota*, and fires were started, although these were soon extinguished. It was now around noon. The two main protagonists had been fighting for 3½ hours. The basic tactical situation remained the same: Jones wanted to attack the *Minnesota*, and Worden wanted to protect her. At that stage the *Monitor* passed close to the stern of the *Virginia*, almost catching her screw for a second time. As the smaller ship passed by, Lieutenant John Taylor Wood fired a 7in. Brooke rifle at the *Monitor's* pilot house. The shell scored a direct hit, blowing off one of the plates that protected the position. When the shell struck, Worden was peering out through the vision slit. The explosion blinded the *Monitor's* captain. Worden fell back, but could still sense the bright light and cool air coming from the hole in the armor. Miraculously, the helmsman was unhurt. Keeler saw "a flash of light and a cloud of smoke." Racing through the ship, he heard the captain call out: "My eyes. I am blind." He called for medical aid, and while Worden lay there, he ordered the helmsman to alter course to starboard, and head for shallow water, where the *Virginia* couldn't follow. He thought the damage to the pilot house was serious enough to break off the fight. Lieutenant Greene arrived, and assumed command. As he was carried below, Worden begged his replacement to "save the *Minnesota* if you can." It was 12.15pm.

The Battle of Drewry's Bluff, 15 May 1862. After nearly four hours, the battered ironclads *Monitor* and *Galena* were forced to retreat, abandoning their attempt to force a route to Richmond by way of the James River. *Harper's Weekly*, 31 May 1862. (Hensley)

Jones guessed something was amiss, and the *Monitor* was running from the fight. On board the *Minnesota*, Van Brunt realized his protector was out of the battle, and he prepared for the worst. The attack never came. The tide was ebbing, and as the water levels went down, the *Minnesota* gained a new protector. The *Virginia* had a draft of 22ft, and the area she could safely operate in was getting smaller by the minute. The pilots argued that the wooden frigate was too far away, and Jones complained that the "pilots will not place us nearer the *Minnesota*, and we cannot run the risk of getting aground again." He could only get within a mile of the enemy frigate, and the tide was still falling. He called his officers together and presented them with the situation. His ship was leaking, the crew was exhausted, and they were unable to fight either the *Monitor* or the *Minnesota*. He proposed a return to Norfolk. Almost all of his officers agreed, although Jones noted: "had there been any sign of the *Monitor*'s willingness to renew the contest we would have remained to fight her". Ramsay said the news was a "wet blanket," and claimed that Jones "ignored the moral effect of leaving the Roads without forcing the *Minnesota* to surrender." Jones ignored his protests, and ordered the helmsman to set a course for Sewell's Point and the mouth of the Elizabeth River. Lieutenant Wood had fired the last shot in the Battle of Hampton Roads.

Both ironclads returned to their respective berths, and were met with a hero's welcome. The *Monitor* had limped from the battleground, but remained undefeated. After four hours of battle, neither ship could claim a victory.

# AFTERMATH

Neither side could claim a victory in the Battle of Hampton Roads. The four-hour battle between the ironclads had been a stalemate. The *Monitor* had been hit 23 times, and the *Virginia* 20 times. Neither ship was badly damaged in the engagement. Although Lieutenant Worden was badly scarred, he survived, and eventually regained his eyesight. There were no other casualties. The day before, the *Virginia* had destroyed two powerful warships and killed or wounded hundreds of Union sailors. Why did the Union regard the battle as a victory? The threat posed by the *Virginia* had been countered. There was no longer any chance of her being able to break the Union blockade, and the industrial capacity of the North ensured the Union would win any ironclad arms race. The first day of the battle demonstrated the vulnerability of wooden ships, and made them obsolete as warships. It also highlighted the danger facing the Union blockading fleets. The second day ushered in the era of the armored warship, and demonstrated that any hopes the Confederates had entertained of breaking the maritime stranglehold around the Confederacy had been dashed. In a single, four-hour battle, the nature of naval warfare had been changed forever.

In a tactical sense, the *Virginia* still dominated Hampton Roads, and therefore controlled access to the James River. As General McClellan was planning an offensive against Richmond, and planned to use Fort Monroe as his base, the Confederate ironclad was a serious threat. She had won a strategic victory by her very existence. McClellan sought assurances from the Navy Department that the *Monitor* could hold the *Virginia* in check. McClellan moved his planned base of operations to the York River, out of reach of the ironclad. For its part, the Navy Department was reluctant to risk the *Monitor* in battle. Under her new captain, Lieutenant Thomas O. Selfridge, she was modified to incorporate improvements to the pilot house and smokestacks, and she was ordered to keep out of the way of her adversary. For its part, the *Virginia* was repaired, and she was issued with new, specially designed armor-piercing bolts. A new and improved ram was also fitted to her bow, and the missing gun port lids were finally fitted. As Buchanan was in hospital, Flag Officer Josiah Tattnal arrived to hoist his flag in the ironclad on 21 March. He was more than willing to renew the fight. Work also began on another casemate ironclad in the Norfolk Yard. Buchanan and Jones were both aware that the *Monitor* had proven to be the equal of the *Virginia*, but neither Tattnal, the Confederate Navy Department, the press, nor the Southern public would hear of it. For them, the *Virginia* was still the victor of the battle, and would eventually prevail over her opponents. Tattnal's orders were to "Strike when, how and where your judgment may dictate." On 4 April 1862, the *Virginia* was ready to reenter the fray, and Secretary of the Navy Stephen Mallory

Confederate Flag Officers Buchanan (left) and Tattnal pictured after the end of the Civil War. Both officers commanded the CSS *Virginia*. From "Battles and Leaders", 1894. (Hensley)

ordered Tattnal to launch an attack on the transports of the Army of the Potomac, which were lying at anchor in Hampton Roads. A week later, on 11 April, the *Virginia* sailed down the Elizabeth River, but the Union transports scattered and ran for the protection of Fort Monroe. Obeying orders to avoid battle, the *Monitor* also fled from Hampton Roads, and headed into Chesapeake Bay. The Union fleet hoped to lure the Confederate ironclad out into deep water, where they could surround her and overwhelm her by sheer numbers. The fleet included the *Vanderbilt*, whose sole purpose was to ram the *Virginia*. Tattnal refused to fall into the trap, and was content with holding Hampton Roads, and the capture of three Union transports. The *Monitor*'s crew was indignant. As one crewman put it, "I believe the Department is going to build us a big glass case to put us in for fear of harm coming to us." The *Virginia*'s reign of terror would not last much longer.

On 3 May, the Confederate Army in the Virginia Peninsula abandoned its defensive lines around Yorktown, and slipped away. Faced with overwhelming numbers of Union troops, General Joe Johnston had no option but to retreat. Three days later President Lincoln arrived at Fort Monroe, and on 8 May he discussed the *Virginia* with General Wool. While the President watched, a Union flotilla moved up to Sewell's Point and began shelling the Confederate batteries there. Suddenly the *Virginia* appeared, and the entire Union fleet turned tail and fled. Once again, the *Monitor* chose to flee rather than to fight. According to the *Virginia*'s Lieutenant Wood, "it was the most cowardly exhibition I have ever seen." Lincoln was less than impressed, but General Wool had already planned a second attack. While the *Virginia* was distracted he slipped the new armored gunboat USS *Galena* and a few wooden warships past Newport News and into the James River. The plan was to seal Norfolk off from Richmond. The following afternoon (9 May), under cover of a second naval demonstration, Wool ferried 6,000 men across Chesapeake Bay and landed them at Ocean View, to the east of Willoughby's Spit. A second wave of troops landed the following morning. The Union army now had a divisional-sized force of 10,000 troops in a position to outflank Sewell's Point, and poised to capture Norfolk itself. Although Confederate Major General Benjamin Huger commanded a similar number of troops, they were scattered between several defensive positions on both sides of the Elizabeth River. He had also been recalled to help in the defense of Richmond, and was in the process of abandoning Norfolk. By nightfall General Wool's troops had entered the city. The first the crew of the *Virginia* knew of the retreat came the following morning (10 May), when they noticed the emplacements on nearby Sewell's Point had been abandoned. Huger's retreating army destroyed the Norfolk Navy Yard, and the *Virginia* was left without a base. The ironclad had too deep a draft to escape up the James River to Richmond, although the rest of the flotilla managed to escape. Lieutenant Jones tried to lighten the ironclad, but by 1.00am on 11 May, it became clear the task was impossible. By lightening the ship, Jones had stripped her of most of her armor, which meant she was unable to attack the enemy fleet. Tattnal had no choice but to scuttle his ship. The *Virginia* was run aground off Craney Island, and her crew prepared the ship for destruction. Jones and Wood lit the fuse and rowed away. The once-proud ironclad caught light then exploded. Her

The USS *Monitor* foundered during a gale off Cape Hatteras, North Carolina, early in the morning of 31 December 1862. The sidewheel gunboat USS *Rhode Island* is shown coming to her aid. Note the temporary modification to the ironclad's smokestack, to prevent waves dousing her engines. (Mariners)

crew marched inland in the wake of Huger's army, and their officers cursed the folly of both the army and their administration. The pride of the Confederate Navy had been destroyed.

Richmond seemed to be wide open, and the Union Navy immediately launched an expedition up the James River. The plan was to force their way as far as Richmond. The *Monitor* and the armored gunship *Galena* led the flotilla, and it seemed that nothing could stop them. The Union squadron was halted at Drewry's Bluff, some 15 miles below the Confederate capital. A fort had been built on top of the bluff overlooking the river, and Tattnal's sailors arrived just in time to help crew the heavy guns that had been placed there. The *Jamestown* was scuttled to block the river, and the defenders ranged their guns in just beyond the obstacle. On 15 May, the *Monitor* and *Galena* appeared and came under heavy fire. They soon found the bluff was too high for their guns to shell, while the plunging fire from Drewry's Bluff threatened to pierce the virtually unprotected decks of the Union ironclads. After four hours, the *Monitor* and its consorts limped away. Richmond had been saved.

The *Monitor* remained on the James River throughout McClellan's peninsular campaign, and covered the retreat of the Army of the Potomac. The new threat was the CSS *Richmond*, the ironclad that had been partially built in Norfolk, and then towed to Richmond to be completed. Captain Jeffers was replaced by Commander Bankhead, and on Christmas Day he received orders to steam south to join the blockade off Wilmington. Towed by the sidewheel steamer USS *Rhode Island*, the *Monitor* reached Cape Hatteras before she was overtaken by a storm. By the late evening of 30 December it became clear that the *Monitor* was sinking. The *Rhode Island* was called on to send boats, and Bankhead gave the order to abandon ship. The steamer was still trying to rescue the crew when the *Monitor* sank, taking four officers and 12 men down with her. At 12.30am on 31 December 1862, the second of the two ironclads was no more. Her remains still lie in 220ft of water.

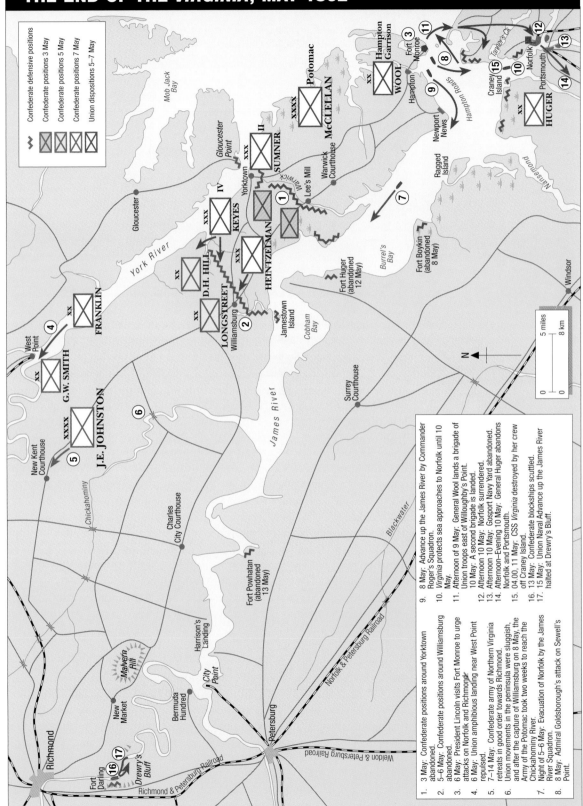

**Legend:**
- Confederate defensive positions
- Confederate positions 3 May
- Confederate positions 5 May
- Confederate positions 7 May
- Union dispositions 5–7 May

Map labels:
- Mob Jack Bay
- Gloucester Point
- Gloucester
- York River
- Yorktown
- Warwick
- Lee's Mill
- Warwick Courthouse
- Newport News
- Ragged Island
- Fort Monroe
- Hampton
- Hampton Roads
- Hampton Garrison
- **WOOL** xx
- **HUGER** xx
- Craney Island
- Norfolk
- Portsmouth
- Nansemond
- Windsor
- **Potomac McCLELLAN** xxxx
- **II SUMNER** xxx
- **IV KEYES** xxx
- **HEINTZELMAN** xxx
- **D.H. HILL** xx
- **LONGSTREET** xx
- Williamsburg
- Jamestown Island
- Cobham Bay
- Burrel's Bay
- Fort Boykin (abandoned 8 May)
- Fort Huger (abandoned 12 May)
- **FRANKLIN** xx
- West Point
- **G.W. SMITH** xx
- **J.E. JOHNSTON** xxxx
- New Kent Courthouse
- Chickahominy
- Charles City Courthouse
- Surrey Courthouse
- James River
- Fort Powhatan (abandoned 13 May)
- Harrison's Landing
- City Point
- Bermuda Hundred
- New Market
- Malvern Hill
- Fort Darling
- Drewry's Bluff
- Richmond
- Petersburg
- Blackwater
- Norfolk & Petersburg Railroad
- Weldon & Petersburg Railroad
- Richmond & Petersburg Railroad

Scale: 0 – 5 miles / 0 – 8 km

N

1. 3 May: Confederate positions around Yorktown abandoned.
2. 5–6 May: Confederate positions around Williamsburg abandoned.
3. 6 May: President Lincoln visits Fort Monroe to urge attacks on Norfolk and Richmond.
4. 6 May: Union amphibious landing near West Point repulsed.
5. 7–14 May: Confederate army of Northern Virginia retreats in good order towards Richmond.
6. Union movements in the peninsula were sluggish, and after the capture of Williamsburg on 8 May, the Army of the Potomac took two weeks to reach the Chickahominy River.
7. Night of 5–6 May: Evacuation of Norfolk by the James River Squadron.
8. 8 May: Admiral Goldsborough's attack on Sewell's Point.
9. 8 May: Advance up the James River by Commander Roger's Squadron.
10. *Virginia* protects sea approaches to Norfolk until 10 May.
11. Afternoon of 9 May: General Wool lands a brigade of Union troops east of Willoughby's Point. 10 May: A second brigade is landed.
12. Afternoon 10 May: Norfolk surrendered.
13. Afternoon 10 May: Gosport Navy Yard abandoned.
14. Afternoon–Evening 10 May: General Huger abandons Norfolk and Portsmouth.
15. 04.00, 11 May: CSS *Virginia* destroyed by her crew off Craney Island.
16. 13 May: Confederate blockships scuttled.
17. 15 May: Union Naval Advance up the James River halted at Drewry's Bluff.

# THE BATTLEFIELD TODAY

Hampton Roads has changed almost beyond recognition over the past 160 years. The only constant is the water itself, dark, deep, and cold. Once a sleepy Tidewater port, Norfolk is now a major American city, and home to what is probably the largest naval base in the world. Much of the shoreline around Sewell's Point and the eastern bank of the Elizabeth River where Confederate soldiers watched the drama unfold is now part of Norfolk Navy complex. In the waters off the point where the *Virginia* spent the night before her battle against the *Monitor*, lines of US Navy supercarriers and amphibious assault ships continue the naval legacy. Further down the river are the berths for smaller vessels: destroyers, frigates, and support vessels. The base is not entirely off limits to the public, although access is still restricted, particularly in the vicinity of Sewell's Point. The US Navy run tours for interested civilians, and the "Norfolk Navy Base Tour Office" is close to the site of the encampment of the Confederate garrison during the spring of 1862. The office can be reached by following Interstate 64 as far as Junction 276C, then following State Road 564 (Admiral Taussig Boulevard) past Base Gate 2. The office is on the right.

**The shore of Newport News Point, looking toward Sewell's Point (now Norfolk Navy Base). The USS *Cumberland* foundered in the shallow waters in the foreground of the picture. (Author's Photograph)**

The Norfolk Navy Yard in Portsmouth, Virginia, still exists as a naval establishment, and is located on the western bank of the Elizabeth River, immediately over the Jordan Bridge, off Route 337 (Elm Avenue). Parts of the shipyard are open to the public, and the Portsmouth Naval Shipyard Museum interprets the history of the base, and the story of the building of the *Merrimac/Virginia*. Of particular interest is a model of the dry dock where the *Merrimac* was converted into the *Virginia*. A pedestrian ferry that runs seven days a week links the site with downtown Norfolk. Visitors to the area should also visit the nearby Lighthouse Museum, which provides a useful insight into maritime activity on the Elizabeth River. The Old Naval Hospital Building is located close to the riverfront at the northern end of Portsmouth, and stands on the site where Flag Officer Buchanan and other Confederate and Union wounded were taken for treatment after the first day's battle. Across the river lies downtown Norfolk, which can be reached by three main Interstates (164, 264, and 464). Interstate 64 serves as a bypass road, linking all three roads with the Hampton Bridge Road Tunnel, one of three major road crossings in the Hampton Roads and Chesapeake Bay area. The museum and maritime science exhibit Nauticus is located on the bank of the Elizabeth River in the southwest corner of downtown Norfolk. On its upper floor it contains a maritime museum dedicated to the naval history of Norfolk and Hampton Roads (The Hampton Roads Naval Museum). A major portion of the museum is devoted to the interpretation of the battle between the ironclads, and contains a full-sized reconstruction of the *Monitor*'s turret, and a cross-section of the *Virginia*'s casemate. Interpretation is augmented by a fascinating collection of artifacts, and an extremely well-presented audio-visual display. While in the area, visitors might consider strolling down through Town Point Park to the river itself, and imagine the scene on that Saturday morning, when thousands lined the shore and silently watched the *Virginia* on her way down the river.

While the Chesapeake Bay Bridge Tunnel links Norfolk with Delaware across the Bay, two other crossings connect Norfolk and Portsmouth with Newport News and Hampton. To the west Route 664 doglegs its way across Hampton Roads, from Pig Point to Newport News Point. To the east of its southern approach is Craney Island, where the *Virginia* was scuttled. The area is now a disposal area run by the US Army Corps of Engineers. The wreck site was located, and artifacts from the *Virginia* are now housed in several collections, including the Museum of the Confederacy in Richmond, Virginia, probably one of the best Civil War museums in the country. The northern end of the crossing is the site where Union batteries fired on the *Virginia* while it attacked the two Union sailing frigates. Once again, the wrecks of both the *Congress* and the *Cumberland* have been located, and artifacts recovered from them are now housed in the Mariners Museum in Newport News, one of the premier maritime collections in the world. Further to the east, Route 64 links Willoughby Spit (now called Willoughby Beach) to Hampton via the Hampton Roads Bridge Tunnel. The bridge itself links the Rip Raps (the site of Fort Wool) with the southern shore, while at the northern end the tunnel emerges immediately to the west of Fort Monroe, located on Old Point Comfort. The fort is open to the public, and contains the Casemate Museum.

**One of a series of interpretative markers located on the shore of Newport News, explaining the events which took place beyond the shoreline to the left a century and a half ago. (Author's Photograph)**

Visitors can reach it by turning east onto Mallory Street (named after the Confederate Secretary of the Navy), then following directions. The museum contains a *Monitor–Merrimac* display (which includes scale models), an interpretation of the history of the fort, and displays dealing with coastal fortifications and artillery. As its name suggests, the museum is located in the inner casemates of the Fort. By driving west from Hampton to Newport News along Chesapeake Avenue, travelers are presented with an excellent view over Hampton Roads, looking out over the piece of water where the two ironclads fought their duel. A series of interpretative signs provides a brief outline of the battle, and shows where certain events took place. Near the western end of the avenue is a small car park, and close by, several signs tell how the *Virginia* destroyed the *Congress* immediately in front of the car park. By standing on the shoreline, you can imagine the scene as the survivors swam ashore, or were rescued in the shallows by Union soldiers. The wreck lies in the mud some 80 yards from the shore. Unfortunately the waterfront in front of the area where the *Cumberland* went down is more commercial, and railroad tracks and the slip-roads onto the Route 664 tunnel and bridge make it difficult to imagine the shore as it looked in 1862. Two museums in the Newport News area are well worth visiting and contain information or artifacts that are relevant to the battle. The Virginia War Museum is situated close to the junction of Route 60 and Mercury Boulevard (leading to the James River Bridge). Incidentally, the bridge crosses the part of the river where the *Virginia* turned around before returning to finish off the *Congress*. The museum covers military activity in Virginia from 1775 to the present day, and provides a venue for the interpretation of the Union batteries and garrisons on the northern bank of Hampton Roads in 1862. Further up Route 60 is the Mariners Museum. Apart from the artifacts from various shipwrecks that have already been mentioned, the museum contains extensive displays of ship models, historical artifacts, and documents relating to the naval side of the American Civil War in general and the Battle of Hampton Roads in particular. It also boasts a world-class book store and gift shop. For researchers, it offers an excellent library and an extensive photo archive.

As for the two ships themselves, the *Virginia* has gone, destroyed by a mixture of treasure hunting, salvage, and dredging operations. Only a handful of artifacts remain in the care of museums in Richmond and Newport News. The Washington Navy Yard in Washington D.C. houses a collection of artillery, including all the guns carried by both of the ironclads during the battle, but the *Virginia's* original guns have been lost. The *Monitor* sank off Hatteras Inlet, North Carolina, in 220ft of water. The site now forms part of an underwater marine sanctuary administered by NOAA (The National Oceanic and Atmospheric Administration). Several artifacts have been raised, and the wreck has been extensively surveyed and the results published. The vessel sank upside down, so the hull rests on her turret. Scientists have recently become concerned for the stability of the wreck, and are considering plans to ease the turret out from beneath the hull in order to preserve it. If the turret and any other part of the ship were raised and conserved, it would provide a direct link with the dramatic events that took place in the waters of Hampton Roads in 1862.

# SELECT BIBLIOGRAPHY

Bauer, Jack K., & Roberts, Stephen, S. *Register of Ships of the US Navy, 1775–1990,*
   Greenwood Press (Westport, CT, 1991)

Bennett, Frank M., *The Steam Navy of the United State*s, Warren and Company
   (Pittsburgh. PA, 1896)

Brophy, Ann, *John Ericsson and the Inventions of War,* Silver Burdett Press (Eaglewood
   Cliffs, NJ, 1991

Canney, Donald L., *Lincoln's Navy; The Ships, Men and Organization, 1861–65,* Conway
   Maritime Press (London, UK, 1998)

Chapelle, Howard I., *The History of the American Sailing Navy* W.W., Norton (New York,
   NY, 1949)

Church, William Conant, *The Life of John Ericsson* [2 volumes], Scribners' Press
   (New York, 1891)

Daly, R.W., *How the Merrimac won: The strategic story of the CSS Virginia,* Crowell Press
   (New York, NY, 1957)

DeKay, James Tertius, *Monitor: The story of the legendary civil war ironclad and the man
   whose invention changed the course of history* Ballantine Books (New York, 1997)

Gardiner, Robert (ed.), *Steam, Steel and Shellfire: The Steam Warship, 1815–1905,*
   Conway Maritime Press and Naval Institute Press (London, UK, and Annapolis, MD,
   1992)

Gentile, Gary, *Ironclad Legacy,* Gentile Productions (Philadelphia, PA, 1993)

Hoehling, A.A., *Thunder at Hampton Roads: The U.S.S. Monitor – Its battle with the
   Merrimack and its recent rediscovery,* Da Capo Press (New York, NY, 1993)

Jones, Virgil Carrington, *The Civil War at Sea* [2 volumes], Rinehart and Winston (New
   York, NY, 1960, reprinted in three volumes by Broadfoot Press, Wilmington, NC, 1990)

Konstam, Angus, *Confederate Ironclad, 1861-65,* Osprey Publishing [New Vanguard
   Series, 41] (Oxford, UK, 2001)

Luraghi, Raimondo*; A History of the Confederate Navy,* Naval Institute Press (Annapolis,
   MD, 1996)

Silverstone, Paul H., *Warships of the Civil War Navies,* Naval Institute Press (Annapolis,
   MD, 1989)

Smith, Gene A., *Iron and Heavy Guns: Duel between the Monitor and Merrimac*
   McWhiney, Foundation Press [Civil War Campaigns and Commanders Series] Abilene,
   TX, 1998)

Stern, Philip Van Doren, *The Confederate Navy: A Pictorial History,* Da Capo Press
   (New York, NY, 1992)

Still, William N.; *Iron Afloat,: The story of the Confederate armorclads,* Vanderbilt
   University Press (Nashville, TN, 1971)

Still, William N. (ed.), *The Confederate Navy; The Ships, Men and Organization, 1861–65,*
   Naval Institute Press and Conway Maritime Press (Annapolis, MD, and London, UK,
   1997)

Underwood, Robert, & Buel, Clarence Clough (eds*.), Battles and Leaders of the Civil War*
   [Volume 1] Century Company (New York, NY 1887), reprinted by Castle, Edison, (NJ,
   1987). **Note.** This source contains articles originally published in *Century Magazine*,
   including accounts by John Ericsson, Dana Greene, Henry Reaney, and others.

Ward, James H., *A manual of Naval Tactics* Appleton and Company (New York, NY, 1859)

West Jr., Richard S., *Gideon Welles: Lincoln's Navy Department,* Bobbs-Merril Company
   (New York, NY, 1943)

White, William Chapman, & White, Ruth, *Tin Can on a Shingle* Dutton Press (New York,
   NY, 1957)

Worden, John Lorimer, *The Monitor and the Merrimac: Both sides of the story,* Harper &
   Brothers (New York, NY and London, 1912)

*Official Records of the Union and Confederate Navies in the War of the Rebellion*
   [30 volumes] Government Printing Office (Washington, DC, 1894–1921)

# INDEX